SEVEN STAR
PRAYING MANTIS KUNG FU

By LEUNG TING

B.A., Ph.D.,
10th Level M.O.C. of I.W.T.L.T.M.A.A.

MATERIALS & CHIEF DEMONSTRATOR
LEE KAM WING
Master of Seven-Star Praying Mantis Style

CHIEF TRANSLATOR
RICHARD LEE
B.A. Hons., M.A., M.I.L.

ASSISTANT TRANSLATOR
BEN LEE

CHIEF EDITOR
LEUNG WAI BUN

ISBN NO. 962-7284-11-4

Printed in Hong Kong

古墨瀋頤卷

PREFACE

uring my recent visit to Europe, people I met in the cities raised the same question to me — "What is kung fu?"

The correct name for kung fu is in fact *"Wu-Shu"*, which means **MARTIAL-ART**. Kung fu is the colloquial term employed by the Chinese people to mean "techniques". Wu-Shu is of course a kind of techniques, and therefore people fall into the habit of calling it **"Kung Fu"**!

In the United States of America, Chinese kung fu has already been taught to kung fu enthusiasts. Nowadays, many people in U.S.A. know that kung fu is only a general term for the art of self-defense or fighting, which in fact includes different systems or styles, known as *"Moon-Pai"* in Chinese.

However, a greater part of citizens in Europe still do not know what "kung fu" means.

In my recent tour to Europe, I met quite a number of self-proclaimed European kung fu *"Sifus"*. These so-called kung fu Sifus are in fact usurping the title of kung fu masters — they are merely *"hanging up a goat's head while selling the dog's meat"*, as the Chinese saying goes. Some of them have but acquired some skills of Karate or Taekwondo, while the rest of them have perhaps read through a few so-called specialized martial-art books *(which can in fact hardly be regarded as specialized)*, or have gone through some training. Having done so, they dare setting up gymnasiums, admitting students, and conferring themselves with titles such as "7th Dan kung fu specialists", or "6th Dan Black Sash". Some even go to the extreme of claiming to be "Founders" of such and such a Style! *(Unfortunely the grading system of Chinese kung fu is completely different from the Japanese grading system; we have NO belt for conferring the degrees, and we NEVER use any sash for this kind of purpose! In fact most of the kung fu styles up to now have NO grading system.)*

Chinese kung fu is a general term. There are in fact numerous styles of Chinese kung fu. Even in the same particular style, it can be divided into different branches. Some branch styles maybe greatly varied, while others maybe less varied.

The most obvious variation in the techniques of one style to another maybe exemplified by the systems of Wing Tsun, Tai Chi, and Choy Lee Fut. Wing Tsun is a system which is characterized by the adoption of flexible techniques, and which prefers making use of the force of an opponent to defeat the opponent himself. This style of kung fu is easily recognised by its narrow stances, and the position of the hands which are often placed in front of the chest to offer it protection. In the Tai Chi Kung Fu, which also prefers making use of an opponent's force to defeat

5

the opponent himself, whereas the stance adopted is much wider than that of Wing Tsun. The range of movement of the arms are similarly wider. In the Choy Lee Fut Style, movements are more vigorous and rigid than those of both Wing Tsun and Tai Chi, and its long bridges and wide stances shows a still greater range of movements of the limbs. That is why an on-looker can easily see the difference among the above three styles if he is watching a show in which the techniques of the above styles are demonstrated.

Some styles may have derived from the same source. Their systems are usually not much different from one and other, and their techniques are partly alike. Examples of this case are the Lama Style, the White Crane Style, and the Hap Gar Kung Fu (or the *Gallant Knight Family Kung Fu*), of which the basic techniques are not much different, because they are derived from the same original system.

Besides, disciples of the same style may have acquired some particular personal experience or attainment, and when they pass their personal experience or attainment to their own students, skills of their respective students may give rise to different branch styles.

An example of this branching off of styles is the Northern Praying Mantis Style, originally a style of Shantung, a province of northern China. But now it has given rise to several branch styles, of which the *Seven-Star Praying Mantis Style* is one.

There are in fact two large systems using the title of Praying Mantis Kung Fu. One is the Northern Praying Mantis System, originated in Shantung Province of the north, and the other is the Southern Praying Mantis Style that came from the Hakka tribe of Kwangtung Province of the south. Although both of them bear the same name, their systems are completely different from each other. Their techniques, stances, forms, theories, even the application of weapons are quite distinct of their own.

Sifu Lee Kam Wing is a famous master of the Seven-Star Praying Mantis Style in Hong Kong. He is also a good friend of mine in the martial-art circle. Nowadays, when many foreign kung fu enthusiasts are not quite clear about what Chinese kung fu really is, I, being a Chinese martial artist, feel that it is my duty to promote, and protect the real Chinese kung fu, I can't allow the so-called master of Chinese kung fu to ruin the portrait of Chinese kung fu. I have a strong desire to introduce REAL Chinese kung fu to the westerners, and to keep them away from kung fu tricksters. This book, the *"Seven-Star Praying Mantis"*, is the first book I write about styles other than my own. But I assure my readers that I shall keep on writing, with my most sincere and serious attitude, books of different styles of Chinese kung fu.

I wish to thank my good friends of the martial-art circle, who keep on giving me encouragement and support. My thanks go particularly to Sifu Lee Kam Wing and his students, who gave me the necessary background materials for writing this book, and his care in helping me in the proof-reading of this book.

Leung Ting

B.A., Ph. D.,

10th Level M.O.C. of Int. Wing Tsun Leung Ting Martial-Art Association.

1 NOV 1979

7

CONTENTS

LEE KAM WING MARTIAL ART SPORTS ASSOCIATION

First Print: April 1980
Second Print: October 1981
Third Print: September 1983
Fourth Print: January 1990
Fifth Print: June 1992
Sixth Print;   September 1994
Seventh Print: March 1999
Eighth Print: October 2002

GRANDMASTER LO KWANG YU

THE ORIGIN & DEVELOPMENT OF THE SEVEN-STAR PRAYING MANTIS STYLE

THE LAST ERA OF THE MING DYNASTY— A PERIOD OF CHAOS

It was said that the **Seven-Star Praying Mantis Style** was created by *Wang Lang* while he was in *Shantung Province* of China. Wang Lang lived in a period when the Ming Dynasty *(1368 – 1644)*, founded by *Chu Yuan Chang*, was at its fall. The country ruled by the Ming government had begun to weaken since the middle of the dynasty. Both external and internal wars broke out and continued until its downfall which took place at the ruling period of Emperor *Si Chung* (year title *Chung Cheng*), who witnessed a fast decline of his country, and widespread resentment of his people.

There was insurrection in many parts of the country, and the government found itself unable to subdue the rebels with its corrupted soldiers. The rebels were gaining in number, as many people, finding their homes and business being destroyed by wars, willingly joined the rebels in order to survive. Eventually, these rebels formed two large bands, one of which was headed by *Li Tsi Cheng*, who finally caused the death of the last Ming emperor.

INTRUSION BY THE MACHUS

Li Tsi Cheng, who forced the last Ming emperor to commit suicide, was

12

however unable to enthrone himself. A military general of the Ming Dynasty, by the name of *Wu San Kuei*, unthinkingly allied with the Manchus and brought the Manchu soldiers into China, with an aim to get back his beloved concubine, who has fallen into the hands of Li Tsi Cheng's rebels, and to clear the rebels from his own path to the throne. The Manchus, who were all the time envious of the vast land of China, swept through the country once they were allowed to pass through the *Shan-Hai Kuan*, the important entry into China mainland. They defeated the rebels, but they also defeated the last enthroned princes of the fallen Ming Dynasty, who offered unsuccessful resistence, and established the Ching Dynasty.

The people of China, being proud to be descendants of the *Han* race, became extremely resentful towards the authoritarian rule of the Manchus. They found the atrocities of the Manchu soldiers unbearable. A feeling of intense nationalism soared in the mind of the Han people. National heroes grieving over the fall of the Ming Dynasty and the loss of the Chinese land to the Manchus, organized activities on the sly to overthrow the Manchu government.

The Manchu government was of course aware of the discontent of the Han people. Ever since their first entry into China, the Manchus never stopped chasing and exterminating the secret armies and secret societies of the national heroes, who at this time could not but go into hiding — some of them went into the mountains and became hermits, some took refuge in monasteries and became monks.

There were different talks about the identity of Wang Lang. Some said he was a Taoist priest, others said he was originally a monk of the Shaolin Monastery. According to sources disclosed by Master Lee Kam Wing, however, Wang Lang should have been an unshaved disciple of the Shaolin Monastery, who later joined the underground members of patriots working for the overthrow of the Ching government and the restoration of the Ming Dynasty.

13

THE FAMOUS SHAOLIN MONASTERY

The *Shaolin Monastery*, situated at *Sung Shan (Mount Sung)*, became famous ever since *Bodhidharma*, the founder of *Zen Buddism* in China, came to China from India during the Liang Dynasty *(503 — 557)*. In the Sung Dynasty *(960 — 1276)*, hearsay was passed down that *"the monks in the Shaolin Monastery knew kung fu!"* This kind of legends, being passed down through hundreds of years, firmly linked the Shaolin Monastery and Chinese kung fu together. As a result, whenever people talk about kung fu, they would inevitably think of the Shaolin Monastery.

The origin of the techniques of the Seven-Star Praying Mantis Style was thus somehow related to the Shaolin Monastery. However, there is no need for us to enquire whether the Shaolin Monastery had a relationship with most of the kung fu techniques of the northern and southern styles of China. As a matter of fact, members of the secret societies in the Ching Dynasty would usually say they were *"graduates of the Shaolin (or, Siu Lam, in Cantonese language, a kind of languages of the southern China) Monastery"* as a way of showing their identities while making contact with others. This term was later adopted by most of the martial-artists of China. That is why even nowadays most kung fu practitioners claimed that their kung fu styles were originated from the Shaolin Monastery.

GRANDMASTER WANG LANG

It was said that Wang Lang was a native of *Tsi Mo District* of Shangtung Province of China. He lived in the period of the fall of the Ming Dynasty and the intrusion of the Manchus, a period of chaos, atrocities, and calamity. Wang Lang was a patriot. However, he realized that conditions at that time were not favourable to him, and that he had to learn and master the best kung fu skills before he could join the other patriots of the secret societies and work for the overthrow of the Manchu government. Bearing this in mind, Wang Lang therefore entered the Shaolin Monastery at Sung Shan in the *Honan Province*.

As the Shaolin Monastery was famous for its martial-art skills, its name was soon made known to the new Manchu government, who became

14

suspicious of its activities, and its relation with the patriotic kung fu practitioners. The Manchus therefore took a close watch on those who associated themselves with monks of the Shaolin Monastery, and, in particular, those who entered the Shaolin Monastery as unshaved disciples for studying kung fu. Wang Lang, seeing that he and the others were being closely watched, understood that he would never realize his ambition, and thus made up his mind to leave the Shaolin Monastery. He roamed about the country, reaching places such as the *O-Mei Mountain,* the *Kun-Lun Mountain*, the *Western Territories (now Sinkiang Province)*, the *Tien Shan (Mt. Tien)*, and all the areas of northern China. During his tour he tried his best to visit the famous masters of kung fu, became their disciples or friends so as to learn & exchange their skills. In this way he had finally acquired the techniques of seventeen kung fu styles. After that he returned to his native place,and settled down in a monastery at *Lao Shan (Mt. Lao)*.

REPEATED DEFEAT

The abbot of the monastery at Lao Shan was found to be the former elder kung fu brother of Wang Lang. Having settled down there, Wang very often practised kung fu with his elder kung fu brother. However, he was again and again defeated by the abbot. Wang Lang realized that he was not skilled enough to defeat his elder kung fu brother, not to mention "defeating the Manchus." He made up his mind to study harder and to overcome his elder kung fu brother someday.

After a long period of hard practice, he was still defeated. The reason was that his *Si-Hing (elder kung fu brother)*, the abbot, was at the same time practising hard everyday. They were thus both improving their own skill. That was why Wang Lang was all the time found inferior in skill to his Si-Hing.

One day, the abbot told Wang Lang that he was going to have a tour, and asked Wang to take charge of the affairs in the monastery during his absence. Wang suspected that his Si-Hing was in fact going away to look for some experts to improve his own skills, and understood that if his Si-Hing succeeded in doing so, he would find it more difficult to defeat him. This thought made him feel very unhappy.

THE MANTIS CATCHING THE CICADA

It was the time of the hot summer, when lychees were ripe, and cicadas were crying among the boughs. One day, Wang Lang went as usual to a clearing in the forest to practise kung fu. After a long time of hard practice, he felt tired and was wet all over from sweating. He sat under a tree to take a rest, while still thinking over ways of defeating his elder kung fu brother. Suddenly, he heard some strange cries of a cicada above his head. He looked up and found that a cicada was being caught by a powerful pair of fore-legs of a mantis. The cicada, though several times greater in size than the mantis, and having a strong pair of fore-legs and a sharp mouth, was helplessly gripped by the mantis, and could only cry piteously.

Wang Lang was first caught with interest by the scene, but later felt pity for the cicada. So he broke off a stalk of a reed, with which he tried to brush away the mantis from the cicada. The mantis, being disturbed, released its prey, and turned towards Wang's reed stalk. It then raised its powerful pair of fore-legs, waving them to challenge Wang for a fight! Wang Lang, seeing that this little insect was so brave, became still more interested in its actions. He then waved the reed stalk to irritate the mantis. The mantis raised its fore-legs to attack the moving reed. The movements of the forelegs of the mantis were so quick and so freely and wilfully controlled that the forelegs succeeded eventually in getting hold of the reed stalk.

HAND-TECHNIQUES OF THE MANTIS

The sight of the techniques of the mantis gave Wang Lang a sudden thought. The technical problem which had all the time boring him was now suddenly solved, not by his own hard practices, but by the little mantis. This sudden discovery made Wang very happy. He then brought the little mantis back to the monastery, played games with it day after day by irritating it with a reed stalk, and carefully watched how the little mantis manipulated the movements of his forelegs in attacks and defence.

After having a careful observation of the movements of the mantis, he systematized the movements of the mantis into a set of techniques, and incorporated this set of techniques with the other seventeen systems of techniques which he had learnt previously, into a fist-fighting system of his own.

STEPS OF THE MONKEYS

These eighteen sets of techniques, when applied in varied combinations, enabled Wang Lang to achieve great progress in his fighting skills. But, in practical application, Wang observed that there were still some weaknesses in his techniques. He then realized that it must be due to the poor co-ordination between his hand techniques and his footwork.

One day, while Wang Lang was walking through a forest path, he saw several monkeys chasing one after the other among the trees. He observed that the monkeys climbed and jumped with high speed because of the free movements of their hind limbs. He suddenly thought of combining the movements of the hind limbs of the monkey and the movements of the forelegs of the mantis. He practised doing this after returning to his monastery, and finally succeeded in creating a system incorporating the foreleg movements of the mantis and the steps of the monkeys, which became the most distinctive characteristic of the **"Northern Praying Mantis Style"**.

Techniques of the Praying Mantis Style — created from an inspiration after observing movements of the forelegs of the mantis and steps of the monkey.

17

VICTORY BY USING THE PRAYING MANTIS TECHNIQUES

Three years passed. During this time Wang Lang practised hard with his newly created techniques, which he learnt from the mantis and the monkey. After careful studies through constant practices and improvements, he systematized his techniques into a *Twelve-keyword Formula, Eight Rigid & Twelve Flexible Movements,* and the *Eight Attacking Points & Eight Non-attacking Points* .... etc.

One day, Wang Lang's elder kung fu brother returned after his long tour. Wang was happy to see him, and passed back to him the management of the affairs of the monastery. After three years' separation, they were both eager to talk about what they saw during these years. From their conversation, Wang Lang knew that his Si-Hing had obtained great improvement on his kung fu techniques. This of course became a greater temptation to Wang, who was all the time waiting to test his own newly created skills, and if possible, to defeat his Si-Hing. Now the long-waited moment had come at last!

The two kung fu brothers then poised their own pre-fighting postures, to get ready for the first competition in three years. To the surprise of the abbot, Wang got the upper hand after a few movements, and kept his elder kung fu brother under complete control in a few rounds with his strange hand-techniques and wonderful steps.

His Si-Hing was astonished not only because he felt he was going to be defeated, but also because he observed that Wang's techniques were much improved, and that his movements were not quite the same as those he showed three years ago. So, he jumped away from the attacking range of Wang, stopped fighting, and offered congratulations to Wang. After that, he asked why Wang had improved so much, and what techniques he had acquired in the past three years.

Wang Lang, though being able to excel his Si-Hing then, dared not boast about what he had learnt in the past three years, bearing in mind that there must still be room for improvement in his techniques. So, he told his Si-Hing in detail how he observed the mantis and the monkeys, and incorporated their movements into his own techniques.

After that incident, the two kung fu brothers strove to study together what they knew and what they had acquired recently. The interchange of knowledge and techniques gave both of them great improvements in their kung fu attainment.

A FIGHTING CONTEST BETWEEN THE FIGHTER OF THE PRAYING MANTIS STYLE & THE FIGHTER OF THE OTHER STYLE

Practitioners of the Northern Praying Mantis Style of China in olden days perhaps never thought of fighting for glory of their style while wearing thick leather headguards, thin boxing gloves, and bodyguards under safty precaution measures. Fighting competitions between two practitioners in ancient time were more often than not cruel "games" in which they were betting on their lives. But nowadays full contact kung fu competitions are conducted under well arranged precautions reducing dangers to the minimum. The picture shows Lee Kam Hoi,*(the left one)*, Sifu Lee Kam Wing's younger brother, having a free fight with a competitioner of another style during a kung fu contest.

19

DEVELOPMENT & SPREAD OF THE STYLE

The Praying Mantis Style, after being created by Wang Lang, developed rapidly and spread far and wide with variations, according to personal attainments of successors, into several branch styles, such as the **Seven-Star Praying Mantis**, the **Plum-Blossom Praying Mantis**, the **Six Combinations** *(or Lu Ho — the Internal 3 Combinations & External 3 Combinations)* **Praying Mantis**, the **Flat Plate** *(also known as the Spotless)* **Praying Mantis**, the **Secret Door Praying Mantis**, the **Jade Ring** *(or known as Yu-Huan — a beauty of the Tang Dynasty)* **Praying Mantis**, the **Dragging-Hand Praying Mantis**, the **Eight-Step Praying Mantis**, the **Leg-Detecting** *(or Tàn Tui)* **Praying Mantis**, the **Tai Chi** *(Great Ultimate)* **Praying Mantis**, and the **Rigid Praying Mantis Style**,... etc.

Generally speaking, the basic movements and sequence of actions of all these branches are not much different from one style to another. But each of these branch styles excel the others in their own characteristics in tactics of fight-verbal formula, application of strength and theories, which become unique in individual Praying Mantis styles. For instance, the Seven-Star Praying Mantis is characterized by its application of the *Seven-Star Steps;* the Plum-Blossom Praying Mantis Style is characterized by the application of three or five chain-punches like the *"Five Petals of the Plum-Blossom";* the Lu Ho Praying Mantis advocates application of flexible force; the Flat Plate Praying Mantis gets its name by the bending of the practitioner's fingers close to the palm while the whole palm is being kept flat; the Secret Door *(or Secret Family)* Praying Mantis Style stresses close-body & short-range attacks with elbows while posing a low stance, and thus taking practice in the *"Body-Separating Eight Elbow-Strikes"* techniques as its most important training course; the Yu-Huan Praying Mantis stresses application of the variation of the *"Jade Ring Steps",* the Dragging-Hand Praying Mantis Style stresses movements such as *"Dragging"* and *"Sliding-grapple"* techniques; the Eight-Step Praying Mantis excels in movements such as *"Tagging",* *"Clinging",* *"Sticking",* and *"Leaning",* and its techniques are application according to theories of the *"Eight Trigrams" (Pa-Kwa)*; the Leg-Detecting Praying Mantis Places stresses on the techniques of kicks and footwork; the Tai Chi Praying Mantis absorbs into its theories principles of the *"Great Ultimate"; (Tai Chi)* the Rigid Praying Mantis Style, as its name implies, stresses the application of powerful heavy striking movements.

HOW THE SEVEN-STAR PRAYING MANTIS STYLE GETS ITS NAME

There are numerous novelized sayings about the nomenclature of the Seven-Star Praying Mantis Style, which come from various sources. But in the author's point of view, the name might have just come from a mere hearsay.

The following are some of the most popular stories about the origin of the name of the Seven-Star Praying Mantis:

At the beginning, when the Praying Mantis Style was first created by its founder Wang Lang, or when it was passed to one of his early successors, the style was simply known as the *"Praying Mantis Style"*, and it had not yet branched off into subsidiary styles. However, the forerunner of this style wanted to spread his techniques into several styles, so he ordered his three disciples to go to the countryside, and asked each of them to bring back a live mantis. The forerunner would then give each of them a name for a style according to the stripes or spots on the wings of their mantis. It happened that one disciple had brought back a mantis having seven spots on its back, arranged in the form of the seven stars. So the forerunner called it the Seven-Star Praying Mantis. Another disciple brought back a mantis having five spots arranged in the pattern of the petals of a plum-blossom, so he called it the Plum-Blossom Praying Mantis Style. The mantis of the third disciple was however spotless, and so he called it the Spotless *(or later transformed to be known as the Flat Plate)* Praying Mantis Style.

Another retold story about the nomenclature of the Seven-Star Praying Mantis Style bears political colours. The tale tells that the forerunner of this style, while all the time hoping to overthrow the Manchus and to restore the Ming Dynasty, called his style the Seven-Star Mantis, meaning that followers of his style would be able to spread as far and wide as the Seven Stars are spread across the sky, which can be seen even in a moonless night, and that all followers of this style, no matter where they are, would work for the downfall of the Ching Dynasty.

Sifu Lee Kam Wing is one among those who believers more in the latter saying, but he adds that the name might have come as a result of all hand-techniques of this style are supported by the basic form of steps, known as the Seven-Star Steps, which would probably have derived from steps resembling the distribution pattern of the Seven Stars. This can be regarded as the most credible explanation about the origin of the name.

SUCCESSORS OF THE SEVEN-STAR PRAYING MANTIS AFTER WANG LANG

The first generation successor of the Seven-Star Praying Mantis Style, who inherited the techniques from the founder Wang Lang, was Taoist Master *Sheng Hsiao*. Master Sheng Hsiao later passed the techniques to *Li San Tsien*, who ran an escort service bureau at *Chi-Nan* in Shantung Province, and was well known for mastery of kung fu techniques in the vicinity.

Li San Tsien, the second generation successor, encounted *Wang Yung Sang* in *Fu Shan District*, and adopted him as his disciple. Wang Yung Sang later passed the civil service examination and was conferred with the title of Third Degree Graduate of Martial-Art.

The fourth general successor was *Fan Yu Tung*, who inherited the techniques less than a hundred years ago. Later Fan Yu Tung passed the techniques to *Lo Kwang Yu*. However, it must be noted that during the period of two hundred ninety years from Wang Lang the founder to Lo Kwang Yu the fifth generation successor, the techniques of the Seven-Star Praying Mantis Style were spread in the restricted area of Shantung only, though Lo himself did spread them in the last fifty years to some parts of northern China.

In 1930, directors of the *Ching Wu Athletic Association*, the head office of which was first set up in *Shanghai*, decided to send Sifu Lo Kwang Yu to come south to promote affairs of its branch association in Hong Kong. This was the first time when techniques of the Seven-Star Praying Mantis Style were brought to Hong Kong.

SIFU CHIU CHI MAN, THE SIXTH GENERATION SICCESSOR

Grandmaster Lo Kwang Yu, known

Picture at right: The late Grandmaster Lo Kwang Yu demonstrating the movement known as "The mantis Catching the Cicada".

as one of the *"Four Elders of the Ching Wu Athletic Association"*, was a respected master, who held an important position in the assocaition.

The news that one of the Four Elders of the Ching Wu Athletic Association had come to Hong Kong to offer tuitions in kung fu made a bustle at the moment, and attracted many young kung fu enthusiasts of Hong Kong, who were eager to learn techniques of the north.

Among the students, one in particular, who was then learn-ing *Tai Chi Chuen, Eagle-Claw,* and *Tam Tui* kung fu at the Ching Wu Athletic Association, was overjoyed at the news of Grandmaster Lo Kwang Yu's arrival.

On the day of Grandmaster Lo Kwang Yu's arrival, this student of the Ching Wu Athletic Assoiation, who turned out later to be **Chiu Chi Man**, was happy and eager to have a look of the new visitor. There was another person, who was equally happy to meet Grandmaster Lo Kwang Yu. He was Chiu's instructor, a Sifu of Tai Chi Chuen in the

Besides fist-fighting techniques, there are, in the Northern Praying Mantis Style, other techniques of weapons also. The picture shows Sifu Lee Kam Wing demonstrating the "Turning Stance Throat Choking" Movement, a movement of the pole techniques of the system. The picture was taken while Lee was still under coaching in the school of his mentor.

The late Grandmaster Lo Kwang Yu *(sitting)* and Grandmaster Chiu Chi Man *(standing at the back)*.

25

A MEMORABLE PICUTRE
Besides being skilled in the techniques of the Seven-Star Praying Mantis Style, Sifu Lee was also an expert of Lion Dancing, and a skilful drummer of the Lion Dancers team. In Hong Kong, Sifu Lee's lion dancers team is well known. This picture shows Sifu Lee offering his lion dancing show in a celebration party of the Hong Kong General Association of the Weaving Industry.

association. It was this instructor who later encouraged and recommended Chiu Chi Man to follow Grandmaster Lo to study the Seven-Star Praying Mantis Style. Therefore it can be said that Chiu Chi Man's mastery of the techniques of the Seven-Star Praying Mantis Style was solely due to his former instructor's patronage.

Chiu Chi Man later passed his techniques to *Lee Kam Wing*, who is introduced to the readers through this book.

26

DEVELOPMENT & SPREAD OF THE STYLE IN HONG KONG

Chiu Chi Man followed Grandmaster Lo Kwang Yu for several years, during which he helped his Si-Fu in managing the classes, and sometimes took over some of the teaching lessons of his master. In the year 1938, when Hong Kong was suffering from an economic frustration, the Hong Kong Branch of the Ching Wu Athletic Association was closed down. However, Chiu Chi Man was not at all discouraged. He invited some kung fu brothers to work together and set up a new association by the name of the *"Man Keung Athletic Association"*. When this association was founded, Chiu Chi Man was elected the first chairman of the executive committee of the association, while Grandmaster Lo was appointed the Chief Instructor.

Some time later, the Pacific War broke out. Hong Kong was then occupied by the Japanese soldiers, and the association was forced to close down. Grandmaster Lo Kwang Yu then returned to his native place in Shantung.

Some time later, Grandmaster Lo died at his native place. When the news of his death reached Hong Kong, all the several hundred students learning the techniques of his style felt extremely miserable.

After the war, Hong Kong, this war-baptized city, was able to recover gradually from the destructions of war, and its economy began to grow from its ruins. As for Grandmaster Lo Kwang Yu's students, most of them had abandoned their profession of kung fu practitioners, and had become merchants. Few of them still engaged in teaching kung fu for a living. Among these few was Chiu Chi Man, who was all the time thinking of his mentor, Sifu Lo Kwang Yu. To commemorate his master's kindness in teaching him, he made up his mind to glorify his style and spread the techniques he learnt from his master.

At present, Master Chiu Chi Man is still regarded as the most energetic promoter of the Seven-Star Praying Mantis Style.

MASTER LEE KAM WING.

ABOUT MASTER LEE KAM WING

aster Lee Kam Wing was brought up in a family of generations of martial artists. His father was a disciple of the Pak Mei Style, and was expertised in its techniques. Thus Lee Kam Wing was educated in kung fu since he was a boy. .

Kee Kam Wing's father Lee Chau, though an expert of techniques of the Pak Mei Style, did not set up any school to admit disciples. In stead, he paid attention to his profession as a merchant. In his leisure hours, he practised Pak Mei Kung Fu just for keeping health. Lee Kam Wing, then a young son of Lee Chau, was eager to learn his father's techniques, but, owing to the fact that his father was a busy merchant, he was not taught enough kung fu techniques directly. However, he did learn lots of techniques as he watched his father and some of his father's kung fu brothers during practices.

Lee Chau opened a small dyeing factory, and, to save expenses, he ordered his son Lee Kam Wing to be his assistant for managing the factory. Lee Kam Wing, being his father's eldest son, was aware of his burden. At that moment, he had just completed his primary education, so he requested his father to allow him to pursue part-time education in a secondary school, while spending part of his time helping his father in the factory.

But Lee Kam Wing had something in mind. He was all the time longing to learn kung fu. He was eager to find a good master of martial arts, whom he might follow.

In 1962, one of Lee Kam Wing's maternal uncles introduced him to Master Chiu Chi Man, a famous tutor of the Seven-Star Praying Mantis Style. Sifu Chiu Chi Man, a favourite disciple of the late Grandmaster Lo Kwang Yu, was highly rated for his techniques. However, Sifu Chiu Chi Man was quite selective in admitting students. He, like many other Chinese kung fu experts, had the traditional idea of being unwilling to teach all his own techniques to everyone of his disciples.

For this reason, Lee Kam Wing, though having become a student of Master Chiu Chi Man at age of fifteen, had to spend ten whole years in his instructor's gymnasium to learn all the techniques.

People of western countries would wonder why a kung fu student has to stay in a gymnasium for such a long period in order to learn the techniques of a kung fu style. However, in the mind of a Chinese student, such a period of study is well spent, as Sifu Lee Kam Wing told the author, "I think it was worthwhile for me to have spent that long period to follow my master, though I have now an idea that to shorten the period of study is a necessary measure for educating young men in the modern world today for the sake of effeciency. However, the traditional method of long-period personal couching still retains it's advantages."

"The old traditional method," he continued, "is a philosophical method, which allows both the teacher and the student himself to test the student's patience and perserverence in his studies. The long period of study is set to allow the student to build up his strength and power of endurance, and to enable him to acquire highly sophisticated techniques which can't be snatched in a hurry."

"As for the tradition of a teacher's unwillingness to teach all his skills to his student," Sifu Lee Kam Wing commented, "the reason might have been that masters of olden days thought that once they had taught their unique skills to their students, these skills might become a tool of vicious - minded students for killing, and such a tool was invisible and fatal! If this happened, it would mean a breach of the martial-art spirit for health and self-defence purposes. On the other hand, a vicious student, who has so easily obtained the unique techniques from his teacher and his style. This would of course ruin the spirit of *"respecting one's teacher and having a feeling of honour for one's style of techniques"*. Therefore, the old masters of Chinese kung fu, who refrained from passing all their techniques to their students, were in fact excusable."

Though Sifu Lee Kam Wing sympathizes kung fu instructors who use the traditional method of teaching, yet his own method of teaching his student is quite scientific and modernized.

In 1972, Lee Kam Wing, being encouraged by his instructor, set up his

30

Picture showing Gradmaster Chiu Chi Man *(sitting)* and Sifu Lee Kam Wing *(standing at the back)*, taken at the time when Sifu Lee was about to complete his course of training under his mentor.

own gymnasium and began to admit students. For the sake of saving students' time of studying and admitting more disciples, he began abandoning the traditional teaching method. He adopted a promotive system for his students, courses of study are divided into grades according to degrees of difficulty. This makes it easy for a student to obtain success in a certain grade of studies, and thus raises the student's interest in their studies.

While teaching in his own gymnasium, Sifu Lee discards the old method of too much emphasizing on teaching students various sets of boxing form. For this method will cause them to have the habit of paying too much attention to the outward look of movements and thus neglecting their practical effect. However, Sifu Lee does not abandon the original patterns of techniques or boxing forms of the Seven-Star Praying Mantis Style at his own discretion, for these patterns still possess their traditional advantages. He feels that many instructors fail in picking out the good points of these patterns and leaving out their weak points. Instead, they allow their students to memorize them all. On the other hand, some instructors wrongly apply their methods, so that some movements, which are primarily fast and versatile in application, are now taught in a way as if they were heavy and slow movements, thus greatly lowering their effect of practicality.

At present, the courses being studied in Sifu Lee's gymnasium include mostly carefully selected practical movements for individuals, besides traditional boxing forms handed down through generations. Furthermore, emphasis is being placed on exercises in twos, which are practical for real fighting situations.

"I admire the training methods of the Wing Tsun Style," said Sifu Lee Kam Wing, "for the training exercises are programmed to fit real fighting situations, though there are only a few boxing forms in that style. Therefore, in the training programmes of my own gymnasium, I have already extracted some practical fighting techniques of the Seven-Star Praying Mantis Style, and re-organized them into sets of single movements for intensive training for my students, so as to enable them to apply these techniques for real fights."

With years of devoted effort, Sifu Lee has now developed a good foundation for his career in promoting the techniques of his system in Hong Kong and South-East Asia, where his name is well-known to all persons of the Chinese martial-art circle.

 **IGHTING THEORY OF THE SEVEN-STAR PRAYING MANTIS KUNG FU**

(I) TECHNIQUES OF THE SEVEN-STAR PRAYING MANTIS STYLE

The main theories of the **Northern Seven-Star Praying Mantis Style** are embodied in the so-called *"Eighteen Systems"*. These eighteen systems are:

The *"Long Punching"* Form of the First Emperor of Sung Dynasty;
The *"Through Back"* Form of Han Tung;
The *"Enclosing"* Movements of Cheng En;
The *"Short Punching"* Form of Wen Yuen;
The *"Short-range Attacks"* of Ma Chi;
The *"Monkey Form"* Kung Fu of Hsuan Huan;
The *"Leaning On"* Kung Fu of Huang Chien;
The *"Palm Thrust At Face"* Techniques of Mien Shih;
The *"Clasped Hands Through Punch"* of Chin Hsiang;
The *"Grappling & Dragging with Heavy Chopping Fist"* attacking methods of Huai Teh;
The *"Hook, Grapple & Pluck"* Techniques of Liu Hsing;
The *"Rolling-in and Punch at Ear"* Kung Fu of Tan Fang;
The *"Touching and Throwing"* Techniques of Yan Ching;
The Strong *"Alternate Kicks"* of Lin Chung;
The *"Seven Styles Chain-Punches"* Form of Meng Su;
The *"Chopping Punch at Breast"* of Tsui Lien;
The *"Rolling Drag and Punch"* Techniques of Yang Kun;
The *"Praying Mantis Styles"* of Wang Lang as a big Combination.

The above 18 systems, being described in a singing formula in the original Chinese text, are techniques which Wang Lang, the founder of the Seven-Star Praying Mantis Style, had adopted and incorporated into the system of his own style.

* **Author's note:**
   The above verbal description, concerning the names of different kung fu styles and their origins, came from ancient sources, of which authenticity cannot be confirmed, nor can the original forms of these styles be traced. The author tries to write down the verbal description for reference only.

As regards stances of the Seven-Star Praying Mantis Style, there are *EIGHT* main fashions in all. They are:

The Eight Stances: —

八大馬勢（八式）

1. The Horse-Riding Stance;
2. The Hill-Climbing Stance;
3. The Medium Stance;
4. The Collapsing Stance *(Reverse-Bow Stance)*
5. The Circle-Entering Stance;
6. The Seven-Star Stance;
7. The Tiger-Riding Stance;
8. The Leg-Hanging Stance. *(Single-Leg Stance)*

1. 騎馬
2. 登山
3. 中式
4. 吞塌
5. 入環
6. 七星
7. 跨虎
8. 吊馬

* **Author's note:**
Among the above eight stances, the last one, which is described as the Leg-Hanging Stance here as preferred by Sifu Lee, is sometimes substituted with the "Squatting Stance" by some other Northern Praying Mantis martial artists.

TRAINING METHOD OF THE EIGHT STANCES COMBINED WITH HAND TECHNIQUES ON THE WOODEN DUMMY

The following set of training movements is compiled by Master Lee by co-ordinating the Eight Stances with fighting hand techniques. The set is simple but practical. Emphasis is placed on the correct posture of the eight stances, correct use of steps and hand techniques and good correlation between them, while all decorative good-looking but impractical movements have been abandoned.

(Illustration 1 — 8) **"HEAD-ON CHOPPING FIST"** WITH **"HILL-CLIMBING STANCE"**
Sifu Lee posing his prefighting posture, with his right hand in front of his left, while facing the wooden dummy. Then he advances one pace, and circling his right arm in an upward direction close to his body, he launches a Head-on Chopping Fist right at the dummy, while his left hand is holding the third arm of the dummy.

(Illustration 9 — 11) **"SIDE-WAY STRAIGHT FORWARD PUNCH"** WITH **"HORSE-RIDING STANCE"**

After that, Sifu Lee retreats to pose the Horse-Riding Stance, and, circling his right forearm downwards, he launches a Sideway Straight Forward Punch at the mid-level part of the trunk of the wooden dummy.

(Illustration 12 – 16) "GRAPPLING-HAND" WITH "MEDIUM STANCE"

Lee withdraws his right arm, stretches the fingers, and grabs the right arm of the wooden dummy with the Grappling-hand.

(Illustration 17 – 20) "HORIZONTAL CHOPPING PALM" WITH **"SWEEP-KICK"**
Immediately after that, Lee turns to the right, poses a Horizontal Chopping Palm with the left hand, and launches a Sweep-kick at the leg of the dummy.

(Illustration 21 — 31) **"SEVEN-STAR STANCE"**

Lee withdraws his left leg after making the Sweep-kick, and places his left leg in front of his right leg. Then he raises his right leg and quickly stretches it to launch a Slant Stamp-kick at the thigh of the dummy, while his right hand is delivering a Straight Forward Punch.

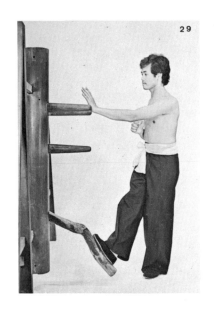

(Illustration 32 – 37) **"INTERCEPT-HAND"** WITH **"TIGER-RIDING STANCE"**

After that Lee moves slightly to his right, posing his left hand in the Intercept-hand Movement, he grabs the left arm of the dummy, while by now he is posing the Tiger-Riding Stance.

(Illustration 38 — 42) "COLLAPSING STANCE", "LEG-HANGING STANCE" & "SLANT SPADE-KICK"

Lee moving his body sidewards to his left, poses the Collaping Stance. Then he raises his right leg to thrust at the "knee-cap" of the dummy with a Slant Spade-kick.

(Illustration 43 — 46) "CIRCLE-ENTERING STANCE"

Lee steps his right foot forwards, and slaps at the third arm of the dummy with his left hand. By now he has posed the Circle-Entering Stance which controls the leg of the dummy. He then launches a right Horizontal Straight Punch at the mid of the dummy.

(Illustration 47 — 50) **"GRAPPLING-HANDS"** & **"MEDIUM STANCE"**
Lee then moves backwards to pose the Medium Stance, while his hands are respectively grappling the right and the third arm of the dummy.

(Illustration 51 — 59) **"HILL-CLIMBING STANCE"**

Lee resumes his Horse-Riding Stance, and then changes it to the Hill-Climbing Stance. He then stretches his right arm to sweep horizontally at the third arm of the dummy. Then he circles it upwards to ward off the right arm of the dummy. After that, he changes it into a Sweeping-hand again to chop the third arm of the dummy.

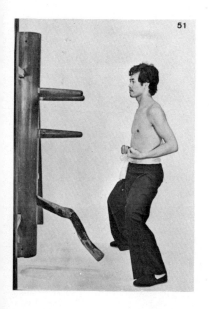

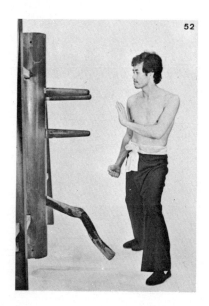

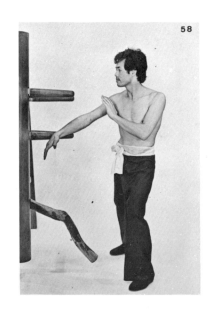

(Illustration 60 — 63) **"INTERCEPT-HAND"** WITH **"SWEEP-KICK"**

Lee's right hand circles upwards to change into an Intercept-hand, while his right leg is being raised to launch a Slant Sweep-kick at the leg of the dummy.

(Illustration 64 – 68) **"INTERCEPT-HAND" WITH "BACK-FLIPPING KICK"**
Lee withdraws his right leg to pose the Leg-Hanging Stance. Then he executes a Back-flipping Kick at the leg of the dummy. After that, he resorts to the Horse-Riding Stance.

(Illustration 69 — 82) **"HILL-CLIMBING STANCE", "INTERCEPT-HAND"** WITH **"SWEEP-KICK"** & **"INTERCEPT-HAND"** WITH **"BACK-FLIPPING KICK"** IN THE REVERSE DIRECTION

Lee resorts to the left Hill-Climbing Stance. Then he repeats the movements as shown above, but in the reverse direction.

END

Fist-fighting techniques can be summarized into the *"Twelve-Keyword Verbal Formula"*. These twelve keywords are:

十二字訣

OU *(Hook)*, 扐
LOU *(Grapple)*, 摟
TSAI *(Pluck)*, 採
KWA *(Upward Block)*, 掛
TIAO-CHIN *(Go forward after Intercept)*, 刁進
PENG-TA *(Chop)*, 崩打
CHAN *(Contact)*, 粘
NIEN *(Cling)*, 黏
TIEH *(Tag)*, 貼
KAO *(Lean)*, 靠
CHIEN-SHAN *(Dodge)*, 欠閃
TENG-NUO *(Bounce)*. 騰挪

*Author's note:
In the Twelve-Keyword Verbal Formula, the keywords OU, LOU, TSAI, KWA, CHAN, NIEN, TIEH and KAO are commonly acknowledged by martial artists of Northern Praying Mantis Styles, while the rest four keywords vary in terminology among different branches and individual practitioners.

For this reason, some martial artists of the Seven-Star Praying Mantis Style agree that the Twelve-Keyword Verbal Formula should be OU, LOU, TSAI, KWA, TIAO (Intercept), CHIN (Go Forward), PENG (Chopping Punch), TA (Attack), CHAN, NIEN, TIEH and KAO. As for the techniques of CHIEN-SHAN (Dodge) and TENG-NUO (Bounce), they are not included in the Twelve-Keyword Formual.

However, the author, after having discussed with Sifu Lee Kam Wing and searching into lots of available sources, finds that there are doubts about the terminology of the above twelve keywords, which do not cover the scope of the techniques of the system. That is why we prefer the set of twelve keywords as described and explained in the book by the author, bearing in mind that this is the personal idea of the author himself, and does not represent the opinion of all the practitioners of the Seven-Star Praying Mantis Style or other branches of the Northern Praying Mantis Style.

THE TWELVE-WORD VERBAL FORMULA

The twelve-word verbal formula of the Seven-Star Praying Mantis Style is synthesized with the keywords *OU (Hook)*, *LOU (Grapple)*, *TSAI (Pluck)*, *KWA (Upward Block)*, *TIAO-CHIN (Go forward after Intercept)*, *PENG-TA (Chop)*, *CHAN (Contact)*, *NIEN (Cling)*, *TIEH (Tag)*, *KAO (Lean)*, *CHIEN-SHAN (Dodge)*, *TENG-NUO (Bounce)*.

Of these twelve techniques, the first eight are applied with emphasis on manipulation of the two hands of the practitioner, while the next three are concerned with movements of the body and footwork. As for the last one, it deals with jumping movements.

The first three keywords, *"Hook – Grapple – Pluck"*, always appear together, as these three techniques are usually applied in co-ordination to serve for both defending and counter-attacking purposes. *"Contact"* & *"Cling"*, *"Tag"* & *"Lean"* form another group of keywords. Of these four, *"Contact"* and *"Cling"* more often than not come to-

gether, while *"Tag"* and *"Lean"* together form a close pair of movements which are too often inseparable. These four techniques, though similar in certain sense, have their respective different functions. *"Dodge"* is a technique made effective mainly with movements of the body and the hindlimbs, in which case skills of the arms and hands are less important. The last keyword *"Bounce"* denotes a technique in which the practitioner bounces up, and, while he is still in the air, makes good use of the moment to launch a kicking attack at the opponent. This is the largest ranged movement among all those implied by the twelve keywords.

Techniques denoted by these twelve keywords and specific ways of applying them are now improved by Sifu Lee Kam Wing, and systematized into training courses offering suitable practices for both individuals and pairs. These training courses are regarded as the most effective for acquiring the techniques of the Seven-Star Praying Mantis Style nowadays.

OU — LOU — TSAI *(Hook — Grapple — Pluck)*

These three keywords usually come together. They denote a group of actions usually applied in sequence, one ofter the other, although neither of these three keywords implies any offensive or counter-attacking movements, yet in real application, there is usually an attacking movement intended — the *Straight Forward-punch* — which eventually comes after the above mentioned movements.

OU (Hook): — The *"Hook"* movement is usually executed with the *TIAO-SHOU (Intercept-hand)*. It is enacted in this way. While the opponent is making an attack with his fist, **the practitioner bends his wrist and makes an outward hooking movement with his palm to deflect the coming fist so as to nullify the punch.** In this case contact is made with the practitioner's palm and the opponent's wrist.

LOU (Grapple): · The word denotes an action which follows that mentioned above. When the practitioner has completed hooking his palm at the opponent's wrist, **he grapples the opponent's elbow with the other hand.** In this

condition the opponent's whole attacking arm is now being under complete control. This is what is meant by *"Grapple"*.

TSAI (Pluck):— When control of the opponent's arm is secured with the movements *"OU"* and *"LOU"*, **the practitioner immediately makes a quick downward drag** (just like plucking a fruit by pulling it away from a branch, as the original word means) thus causing the opponent to lose his balance and fall forward. This is what is meant by *"Pluck"*.

But this is not the end of the practitioner's movements. While the opponent is falling forward, he changes his *"Hook"* movement into a *Straight Forward-punch* to launch a heavy blow at the opponent's face.

The Horse-Riding Stance is considered to be the most basic stance, as all other kinds of stances are derived and modified from it. Most of the exercises described below are carried out while the practitioner is posing the Horse-Riding Stance.

▶

In application of the *TIAO-SHOU*, the force is exerted at the last three fingers — the middle, fourth, and the little finger — to secure a firm grip at the opponent's arm.

TIAO-SHOU (Intercept-hand)

COMBINED EXERCISES OF OU – LOU – TSAI FOR INDIVIDUALS

(Illustration 7 — 12) OU (Hook)

Lee's left hand stretches forward from his side at waist-height to the front of his chest. Then it flaps to the left side, making an outward hooking movement as if trying to claw at something.

(Illustration 13 — 15) **LOU (Grapple)**
Lee stretches his right arm to his front, then stretches wide his fingers. After that he slaps his right hand from right to left.

(Illustration 16 — 17) **TSAI (Pluck)**
Lee postures the fingers of his hand in a way as if having a firm grapple of something. Then he suddenly exerts a downward pull with both hands, just like pulling down a branch for plucking the fruit on it.

(Illustration 18 — 21) **STRAIGHT FORWARD PUNCH**
The Straight Forward Punch is applied in co-ordination with the movement *TSAI* for counter-attacking purposes. It is executed, as shown in the illustration, with the left hand, while the hands have just finished exerting a quick pull.

(Illustration 22 — 32) OU — LOU — TSAI FOR THE RIGHT ARM

Lee withdraws his left arm, and at once makes a sideward flip to the right with the right hand, thus making a movement of the keyword *OU*. Then his left arm executes the *LOU* movement. After that the arms repeat the movements as shown in the previous set of illustrations.

(Illustration 33 — 42) OU — LOU — TSAI MOVEMENTS WHILE FACING THE LEFT
Having completed the above movements, Lee changes his Horse-Riding Stance to the Hill-Climbing Stance, so that he is now facing the left direction. He then repeats the set of movements as described in illustrations 22 to 32.

(Illustration 43 — 55) OU — LOU — TSAI MOVEMENTS WHILE FACING THE RIGHT

After that, Lee withdraws his left fist, as his right hand slips along the lower part of his left arm to make a horizontal flip from left to right while he is turning his stance to the right direction. Then he makes an *OU* movement with the right Intercept-hand. Continuously he repeats the movements as described above.

END

EXERCISE OF OU — LOU — TSAI IN TWOS

When movements of *OU — LOU — TSAI* practices for individuals have become fluent, students should go on to practice of these movements in twos. The following illustrations show movements during practice with partners. In having this training exercise, beginners should note the following points:

1. The movements illustrated below are to be executed in a continuous sequential cycle. Care must be taken to watch the variation of movements so as to keep a smooth cycle.
2. At the movement of *TSAI,* the downward pull is a strong and sudden action, which enables the practitioner to make use of the forward tumbling of the oppnent (when he is losing balance) to execute the Straight Forward Punch which follows.
3. In practice a student should relax his body, and should never exert "Brute Force" to counteract his partner.
4. Movements should be slow during the first few practices, when care should be taken to make good co-ordination with the partner. Later the speed of movements can be increased.

81

And So On......

KWA *(Upward Block)*

This is a movement applied, while the opponent is making a straight punch or a downward chop, in a way that **the practitioner bends the elbow of one arm and raises the horizontal forearm upwards to block the coming attack.** It is meant to deal with heavy attacks, and therefore a great force is being exerted, so it belongs to a movement of the "rigid" type.

As only one arm is needed to apply the *"Upward Block"* for defense, the other arm is now free to launch a Straight Forward-punch at this movement while the opponent's arm is being blocked at the upper level, leaving his middle level unguarded.

EXERCISE OF KWA

FOR INDIVIDUALS

(Illustrations 1 — 7) **LEFT UPWARD BLOCK WITH RIGHT STRAIGHT FORWARD PUNCH**
Lee's left arm stretches forward and raises horizontally to execute an Upward Block. At this moment Lee's right hand launches a Straight Forward Punch.

(Illustration 8 — 14) RIGHT UPWARD BLOCK WITH LEFT FORWARD PUNCH
Then, Lee withdraws his right arm to form a right Upward Block, while at this moment his left arm is lowered to execute a left Straight Forward Punch.

(Illustration 15 — 22) **UPWARD BLOCK WHILE FACING LEFT**
After that, Lee changes his Horse-Riding Stance to the Hill-Climbing Stance, so that he is now facing the left. He then repeats the movements of the Upward Block.

(Illustration 23 — 27) **UPWARD BLOCK WHILE FACING RIGHT**
After that, Lee turns to his right, and repeats the Upward Block movements.

* The above individual exercises are to be
  repeated until they can be mastered fluently.

EXERCISE OF KWA IN TWOS

The exercises of the Upward Block in twos are done while the practitioner applies his alternate left and right Upward Block to counter-act his partner's alternate Round House Punches.

END

TIAO-CHIN *(Go forward after Intercept)*

The phrase means "to intercept, and then go forward to attack" Though it seems that attacking follows intercepting, the two movements can be regarded as a chained action with two arms, first to block, then to counter-attack. In application, the first movement is illusive, while the second movement is a real one.

It is applied in this way. When the opponent makes a punching attack, the practitioner first applies his *TIAO-SHAO (Intercept-hand)* to hook the opponent's wrist so as to deflect his attack. The palm then drags the opponent's arm to the practitioner's side. This movement not only nullifies the opponent's attack, but also causes the opponent to lose balance and fall forward. At this moment the practitioner's hand glides along the opponent's arm to make a counter-attack at the opponent.

EXERCISE OF TIAO-CHIN FOR INDIVIDUALS

(Illustration 1 — 4) **TIAO-SHOU (Intercept-hand)**
Lee stretches the fingers of his left hand and moves his left palm to the left as if trying to grapple something, thus forming the *TIAO-SHOU.*

(Illustration 5 — 8) **GO FORWARD**

After that, Lee stretches the fingers of the left hand again while withdrawing his left hand for a short distance. Then he thrusts his palm forward at high speed with a Straight Forward Stamping Palm.

(Illustration 9 — 10) **WITHDRAWAL**
Lee then withdraws his left arm to his side.

(Illustration 11 — 12) **TURNING STANCE**
Lee stretches his right arm to the front while turning to the right.

(Illustration 13 — 20) **THE RIGHT TIAO-CHIN**
Lee poses a right Intercept-hand at first, and then changes it to the Straight Forward Stamping Palm to thrust forward.

EXERCISE OF TIAO-CHIN IN TWOS

In this exercise, the partner attacks the practitioner with Straight Forward Punches, and the practitioner counter-acts with first the *TIAO (Intercept-hand)*, and then the *CHIN (Go Forward)* movement. These movements can be carried out alternately by the two hands for repeated times over and over again until the pair feel tried.

PENG-TA *(Chop)*

This is a technique enacted by **the co-ordination of the** *TIAO-SHOU (Intercept-hand)* **and the heavy** *Chopping Fist.*

It is applied when the opponent makes an attack. The practitioner of this technique first applies an Intercept-hand to deflect and nullify the attack and cause the opponent to fall forward. Then, taking advantage of the opponent's loss of balance, the practitioner delivers a heavy chopping blow with his other arm.

EXERCISE OF PENG-TA FOR INDIVIDUALS

The *PENG* is the Revese Punch launched by first circling the foearm upwards along the chest, then suddenly thrusting the back of the fist forward-downwards at the opponent. Thus it can be said to be a back-first Chopping Punch. On the other hand, *TA* means to hit or to attack. Therefore *PENG-TA* means to attack the opponent with a Chopping Fist.

104

(Illustration 1 — 3) **TIAO-SHOU**
Lee stretches his left hand to form the *TIAO-SHOU.*

(Illustration 4 — 7) **PENG-TA (CHOP)**
Then, Lee's right fist circles upwards along his chest and chops forward-downwards in the form of a Chopping Fist.

106

(Illustration 8 — 11) **TIAO-SHOU WHILE FACING RIGHT**
After that Lee stretches the fingers of his right hand to form a *TIAO-SHOU* while at the same time he turns to the right.

(Illustration 12 — 15) **PENG-TA**
Lee's left fist chops down.

* *The above movements can be repeated while turning to the left, and vice-versa.*

APPLICATION & EXERCISE OF PENG-TA IN TWOS

The partner launches a right Straight Forward Punch to attack the practitioner. The practitioner immediately applies a right *TIAO-SHOU* to nullify the punch and grapples the attacking arm. Then the practitioner executes a left Chopping Fist to counter-attack his opponent.

COMBINED EXERCISE OF TIAO-CHIN & PENG-TA WITH PART-NERS

* *The training of the keyword TIAO-CHIN and PENG-TA in twos can be combined together to form a double-folded exericse. Started from Pg.102 — 103 photos A to G, we then continuously follow the actions from photo G1 to S.*

(Illustration G1 — S)
The practitioner attacks his partner with a left Straight Forward Stamping Palm, which will be deflected by the partner's right *TIAO-SHOU*. The partner then counter-attacks with a left Straight Forward Punch, which will be nullified by the practitioner's right *TIAO-SHOU* as the punching arm is being grappled. After that the practitioner executes a left Chopping Fist at the head of his partner.

111

CHAN — NIEN *(Contact — Cling)*

The keyword *"Contact"* denotes a condition in which the practitioner comes into physical contact with his opponent. The keyword *"Cling"* denotes a condition of sticking to one's opponent.

Though these two keywords are different in meaning, yet they are closely related to each other, and are very often applied together, as *"Cling"* is impossible without *"Contact"*.

The techniques of *"Contact"* and *"Cling"* are defined as flexible movements, which serve for dissolving the opponent's attack. The importance of these techniques lies in applying them with adeptness, so that when making contact with the opponent's arms, the practitioner can react quickly to nullify his opponent's attack, and sensing the variation's of the opponent's arm movements, the practitioner will be able to make quick changes of his movements to launch counter-attacks.

EXERCISE OF CHAN — NIEN (CONTACT — CLING) FOR INDIVIDUALS

CHAN — NIEN is a set of more complicated successive movements. Therefore students attempting to do these exercises should watch carefully the movements shown in the illustrations. Besides, these movements can be executed in a recurring cycle.

113

(Illustration 1 — 3) **RIGHT TIAO-SHOU**
Lee postures a right *TIAO-SHOU,* and then witdraws it a little close to his side.

(Illustration 4 — 5) **LEFT LOU-SHOU**
After that, Lee stretches his left hand to form a *LOU-SHOU,* which is then slightly lowered.

(Illustration 6 — 7) **RIGHT THRUSTING PALM**
After that, Lee flattens his right palm, keeping the four fingers close together, and then thrusts the palm forward.

(Illustration 8 — 9) **RIGHT LOU-SHOU**
Lee then changes his right Thrusting Palm to a right *TIAO-SHOU* to hook downwards.

(Illustration 10 — 11) **LEFT LOU-SHOU**
Lee again stretches his left hand first to slap, then to grapple and press down.

(Illustration 12) **RIGHT THRUSTING PALM**
Lee's right hand postures the Thrusting Palm.

(Illustration 13 — 15) **LEFT UPPER BLOCKING MOVEMENT**
Lee withdraws his right hand, and raises his left forearm to block upwards.

(Illustration 16 — 18) **RIGHT LOWER THRUSTING PALM**
Lee withdraws his left arm, and places the left palm in front of his chest, while at this moment he flattens his right palm to strike in a forward-downward direction.

(Illustration 19 — 23) **RIGHT TIAO-SHOU**
Lee withdraws his right arm to posture a *TIAO-SHOU* hooking movement.

(Illustration 24 — 25) **LEFT LOU-SHOU**
Lee's left arm enacts the *LOU-SHOU* movement.

(Illustration 26) **RIGHT THRUSTING PALM**
Lee stretches his right hand to enact the Thursting Palm movement.

* The movement as shown in Illustration 26 is then changed back to the movement shown in Illustration 6, and the whole set of movements can then be repeated, thus forming a recurring cycle of CHAN — NIEN.

EXERCISE OF CHAN — NIEN IN TWOS

The *CHAN — NIEN* exercise is a set of movements for developing the sensitivity of limbs. However, if a trainee can well master these movements after a period of severe training, he can apply the techniques in real fights in such a way that his actions will be fluent, adeptly and mechanically controlled through his sense of touch with his opponent's limbs. These are in fact real aims of training in the *CHAN — NIEN*. The following exercise shows a set of sequential movements. Trainees should pay particular attention to the sequence of movements and how each movement changes to another.

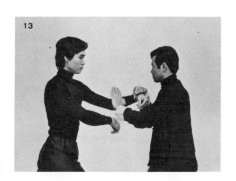

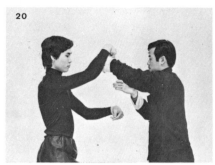

BACK TO PHOTO 8

TIEH – KAO *(Tag – Lean)*

The keyword *"Tag"* denotes an action of closing in, thus shortening the distance between the practitioner and his opponent. The keyword *"Lean"*, on the other hand, means leaning against the oppoent or coming into body contact with the opponent so as to launch attack right at the opponent's side. *"Lean"* is impossible without first applying the technique of *"Tag"*. That is why the two keywords usually come together, and the techniques are applied in succession. Tag and Lean can't be applied with the arms only, but also with footworks, which make fast and vivid steps to make Tag and Lean successful. Therefore, they are a combination of complicated and complex movements.

Into this group of complex movements, Sifu Lee adds the use of the elbow, so that the movements are not only defensive in nature, but are counter-attacking in effect.

EXERCISE OF TIEH – KAO FOR INDIVIDUALS

(Illustration 1 — 2) **RIGHT TIAO-SHOU**
Lee's right hand postures the right Intercept-hand.

(Illustration 3 — 4) **RAISED ELBOW & CROSS-LEG STANCE**
Lee twists his legs to pose the Cross-Leg Stance and raises up both the elbows of his arms, the right one in an Intercept-hand pose, the left one in a fist pose.

(Illustration 5 — 7) **LEFT FORWARD STEP**
Lee's right foot advances one pace to form the Horse-Riding Stance.

(Illustration 8 — 10) **SIDEWAY HORIZONTAL ELBOW-STRIKE**
Instantly, Lee strikes his left elbow sideways, while his right palm presses on his left fist to add force to his left elbow.

Pages 130 — 131 show a set of photos taken at the opposite direction to the demonstrator. These photos show the correct movements of the body, the steps and the Cross-Leg Stance. The above movements illustrate a set of left-handed TIEH — KAO exercises. However, a trainee can follow these photos carefully and duplicate a set of right-handed TIEH — KAO exercises.

APPLICATION OF THE TIEH — KAO MOVEMENTS

The following photos show ways of using the keyword *TIEH — KAO*. Trainees can follow the illustrations and apply them in exercises with partners.

End

133

CHIEN-SHAN *(Dodge)*

This is purely a techniques which involves the use of steps and body movements. In this case the movements of the arms are less important. The purpose of this technique, as the keyword implies, is solely defensive. It should be noted, however, that this technique can deal with very heavy attacks.

Sifu Lee has however added an attacking movement to this technique, thus changing it into a combined movement of both defensive and counter-attacking in nature, and therefore strengthening its original effect.

EXERCISE OF CHIEN-SHAN FOR INDIVUDALS

(Illustration 1 — 7)
Lee poses the Tiger-Riding Stance. He then suddenly moves his left leg to his left, turning his trunk to the left, while he is looking to the right. Then he poses the Tiger-Riding Stance. At this moment he launches a right Straight Forward Punch.

(Illustration 8 — 12)
After that, Lee moves his right leg, turns his trunk to the right, while he is looking to the left and posing the Tiger-Riding Stance. At this moment he launches the left Straight Forward Punch.

APPLICATION & EXERCISE OF CHIEN-SHAN IN TWOS

The following photos show ways of application of *CHIEN-SHAN* and exercise in twos. *Illustration 1 — 6* are the whole set of the *CHIEN-SHAN* movements, which are the same as applied in real fights. However, for daily exercises in twos, the movement shows in *Photo 5* should be followed by those shown in *photos 6A, 7, 8, 9, 10, 11* and *12.*

(Illustration 1 — 3)
The practitioner dodges to the right side of his partner when the later launches a right Straight Forward Punch to him.

(Illustration 4 — 6)
The practitioner then delivers a right Straight Forward Punch at his partner.

(Illustration 6A — 7)
However, before the practitioner's right Straight Forward Punch takes its effect, the partner immediately changes his right punching fist to a Grappling-hand to catch and control the practitioner's right punching arm.

(Illustration 8 — 9)
When the partner intends to launch a left Straight Forward Punch again, the practitioner, with the help of his left Pressing-hand, frees his right arm from the partner's grapple, and then dodges to the partner's left side.

(Illustration 10 — 12)
The practitioner slaps away the punching fist and then counter-attacks with a left Straight Forward Punch aiming at his partner's left flank.

138

End

TENG-NUO *(Bounce)*

The keyword *"Bounce"* **denotes a technique of jumping from which an attacking movement is derived.**

Sifu Lee has incorporated this technique into a set of training exercises, in which the technique of bouncing is modified to include an offensive kicking movement together with an arm-controlling movement. Generally speaking, *"Bounce"* is a large movement which is meant to be applied while the practitioner is at comparatively a greater distance from his opponent. Lack of a suitable distance and an opportunate chance of securing an effective attack will render application of this technique difficult and impracticable.

EXERCISE OF TENG-NUO FOR INDIVIDUALS

The following set of movements, which bears a high degree of difficulty, is quite complicated. Beginners are advised to pay great care in observing the movements shown in the following photos, and do the exercise slowly.

1. *Illustrations 1 — 3* show the moment the practitioner kicking up his left leg before he kicks up his right leg, so as to enable himself to jump higher.
2. *Illiustrations 6 — 7* show the movement of the Two-Finger Strike. Trainees should pay attention to the timely co-ordination of the striking movement with the kicking movement.
3. Please pay attention to the hands, and their relative positions as shown in *illustrations 6 — 11.*

(Illustration 1 -- 6)

Lee hops on his left leg, and bounces up while kicking out his right foot, at the same time strikes out two fingers of his right hand. When his left foot touches the ground, he withdraws his right leg and right hand.

(Illustration 9 — 12)
After that, Lee bounces up again and moves both his hands from left to right along a curve, as if grappling something.

(Illustration 13)
Lee kicks out his left foot at a low position.
(Illustration 14)
Lee returns to his original position, and resumes his Prefighting Hand Posture of *"The Mantis Catching the Cicada"*

EXERCISE & APPLICATION OF TENG-NUO IN TWOS

When the partner initates a right Straight Forward Punch at the practitioner, the latter grapples the partner's arm with his own hands. And, taking the partner's arm as support, the practitioner bounces up to launch a right kick at the partner's throat *(or chest, which in this case, is known as the Chest-Piercing Kick)*. At the same time he attacks the eyes of the partner with the Two-Finger Strike, which is enacted by his index finger and his middle finger *(This technique is known as Two Dragons Snatching the Pearls)*. When the practitioner withdraws his right leg, he grapples the partner's arm for the second time, and immediately after that, he kicks his left foot at the partner's groin — a movement known as *"Kick at the Groin"*.

* Author's note:
The so called "Two Dragons Snatching the Pearls", "Throat Piercing Kick" (or Chest Piercing Kick) and "Kick at the Groin" in the Seven-Star Praying Mantis Style are cruel and fatal movements. During exercises, these movements should be handle with the greatest care for the sake of safety!

147

(II) TRAINING IN THE TECHNIQUES OF THE SEVEN-STAR PRAYING MANTIS STYLE

To be successful in benefiting oneself from training in the techniques of the Seven-Star Praying Mantis Style, a beginner should first learn the principles of the *"Five Internal Elements"* and the *"Five External Elements"*, and the co-ordination between these two groups.

The *Five Internal Elements* are:　　　　　　內五形

1. Energy　　　　　　　　　　　　1. 精
2. Spirit　　　　　　　　　　　　　2. 神
3. Respiratory Strength　　　　　　3. 氣
4. Force　　　　　　　　　　　　　4. 力
5. Power of Attainment　　　　　　5. 功

Energy is meant to be full and resourceful;
Spirit is meant to be high;
Respiration should be smooth and deep;
Force is to be great and enduring.
All these four conditions will come only as a result of acquisition of *"Power of Attainment"*.
On the other hand, *Power of Attainment* is increased from constant abidance by the above four elements through persistent training.

The *Five External Elements* are:　　　　外五形

1. The Hands　　　　　　　　　　1. 手
2. The Eyes　　　　　　　　　　　2. 眼
3. The Body　　　　　　　　　　　3. 身
4. Methods of Application　　　　　4. 法
5. Footwork　　　　　　　　　　　5. 步

Eyes should be sharp-sighted;
Hands should be moving at free will;
The Body should be relaxed;
Footwork should be fast and in vivid steps.

148

All these parts of the body should be moving in accordance with *Methods of Application* as required at different moments and in different instances.

There should be harmony between the *"Five Internal Elements"* and the *"Five External Elements"*. *Power of Attainment* and *Methods of Application* should be improved at the same time through training and constant practices. The learner can acquire techniques of the Seven-Star Praying Mantis Style and reach a high standard of attainment only when he has successfully accomplished the above requirements.

The ultimate objective of training in the techniques of the Seven-Star Praying Mantis Style is to acquire the so called *"Three Speeds"* and the *"Three Attainments"*.

The Three Speeds 三快
Speed of the Hands — This will enable the practitioner, while being offensive, to take advantage of his opponent by rendering surprise attack, and, while on the defensive side, to make fast variations of movements to cope with various attacks by the opponent.

Speed of the Steps — This will enable the practitioner to advance or to retreat as fast as he wishes or as required.

Speed of the Feet —This in fact means fast kicking movements. A kick will be effective in wounding the opponent only if they are fast enough. Though the opponent might have noticed a kick, yet he might not have enough time to avoid it if it is fast.

The Three Attainments 三到
Attainment of the heart — In this context, the heart means the mind. It is the mind which makes a thought, and which controls movements of the body. A practitioner, who has a quick mind, can control movements of his limbs and can thus easily apply the techniques he has learnt. To do this he must try to concentrate his mind both when practising and when being engaged in a real encounter with an opponent.

149

Attainment of the Eyes — It is the eyes that convey to the mind what is being seen. This stimulus of sight will cause a reaction from the mind, which then directs movements of the limbs. To apply this process to kung fu, a practitioner should carefully watch movements of his opponent, so as not to be taken by surprise. He should be observant, so as to see the weak points of his opponent, and whether an attack movement is real or false. His mind should be able to predict correctly what his opponent is going to do at that moment, and what he will do next. Then the practitioner will be able to have suitable reactions with his limbs, and to take up a suitable position, or to keep himself at a suitable distance from his opponent.

Attainment of the Hands — The eyes convey what is being seen to the mind. The mind makes a decision that causes certain reaction with the limbs. Movements of the limbs should be quick, accurate but variable. Quick actions without accuracy are simply fruitless. A slight mistake in the movements will render them to be ineffective. Movements with mistakes, though slight, will bring failure to the practitioner, and will fail him in achieving *"Attainment of the Hands".*

In practice, if a practitioner can achieve the *"Three Speeds",* he will be able to attack with his hands or with kicks just enough to overcome his enemy, and to advance or retreat for his own advantage. In addition to the *"Three Speeds",* if he has acquired the *"Three Attainments",* he can have good co-ordination between the eyes and his limbs, as his mind thinks quickly and correlates them well. At this stage, the practitioner should be able to act accurately, not to make vague movements, and not to launch ineffective kicks. He will not be taken in by his opponent's tricks. He will not be confused by his opponent's movements. He knows what his opponent will do and what he himself should do. He is sure to beat his opponent.

(III) FIGHTING METHODS

A practitioner of the Seven-Star Praying Mantis Style, once being confronted by an opponent, will adhere to a set of principles, which are summarized into the following verbal formulae:

METHODS FOR APPLICATION OF FIGHTING TECHNIQUES:—
The Eight Rigid Methods
The Twelve Flexible Methods

METHODS FOR PSYCHOLOGICAL PREPARATION:—
The Three Conditions of Stability

WEAK POINTS OF THE HUMAN-BODY:—
The Eight Attacking Points
The Eight Non-Attacking Points

"The Eight Rigid Methods"

1. The Mountain Tai Coming Down Onto the Head.
2. Front Straight Forward Punch at the Face.
3. Double Palming Attack with Forward Step.
4. Elbowing Hard with Joined Hands.
5. Leaning Forward Against Door & Wall.
6. Heavy Chopping Fist with Surprising Lower Attack.
7. Left & Right Alternate Round House Punches.
8. Grapple, Drag and Ward Off.

八剛	1.泰山壓頂	5.貼門靠壁
	2.迎面直統	6.硬崩底伏
	3.順步雙掌	7.左右雙運
	4.叠肘硬拱	8.捽捋兩分

*** Author's note:**
In the theories of the Seven-Star Praying Mantis Style, the term "KANG" (Rigidity) means the application of a straight-forward powerful force mainly for attacking purposes. The aim of applying such a force is for immediately defeat of the opponent at one action. The following are examples of applying the so called Eight Rigid Methods.

The Mountain Tai Coming Down Onto the Head:—
Sifu Lee stands face to face with his opponent. The opponent launches a left Straight Forward Punch at Lee. Lee slightly dodges to his opponent's left side, and grapples the opponent's arm with his left Intercept-hand, and at the same time executes a powful Slant Chopping Fist at the opponent, thus seriously wounding the back of his neck.

Front Straight Forward Punch at the Face:—
Having stopped the opponent's Straight Forward Punch with an Upper Block, Lee returns his opponent with a strong Straight Forward Punch aiming at the opponent's face. *(*It should be noted that no matter with what movements the practitioner counters his opponent, whenever he delivers a Straight Forward Punch, it must be executed with a powerful force!)*

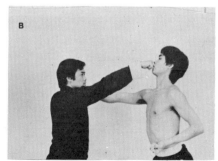

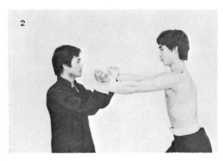

Elbowing Hard with Joined Hands:—

Lee stands facing his opponent. The opponent's left hand suddenly grapples Lee's left wrist.
Lee returns him with the same technique, by posing his left hand in an Intercept-hand to hook
at the opponent's wrist. At the same time he advances a pace, joining his two hands, he uses
his right elbow to press down his opponent's arm. Having depressed his arm, Lee at once
executes a right Reverse Chopping Fist attack at the back of his opponent's neck.

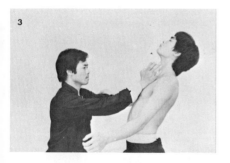

Double Palming Attack with Forward Step:—
Having dissolved the opponent's attack, Lee steps forward while launching his Double Stamping Palms attack at his opponent.

Leaning Against Door & Wall:—
Lee intercepts the opponent's coming Straight Forward Punch with his right arm. After that, Lee advances one pace, and allows his left palm to have a firm grip of his own right arm, thus joining his two arms and forming a strong force, with which he presses hard on his opponent. Instantly he poses a Circle-Entering Stance by inserting one leg behind the opponent's front leg and uses his own knee to lean against the opponent's front leg so as to force it falling downwards. By the co-ordination of the arms and the stance Lee powerfully presses his opponent to lose balance and fall backwards.

Heavy Chopping Fist with Surprising Lower Attack:—
When the opponent launches a right Straight Forward Punch at Lee, Lee wards it off with his left hand, and presses down the opponet's attacking hand. After that Lee's right hand changes to a Chopping Fist to attack the opponent's head, while his right leg is launching a kick at the opponent's groin.

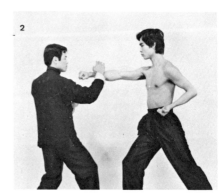

Left & Right Alternate Round House Punches:—

As the opponent is launching a right Straight Forward Punch at Lee, he wards off the punch, and presses it down with his right hand. Immediately after that, Lee's left fist travels along a curve line to strike at the opponent's right temple. The strike being effectuated, Lee continues to launch attack by grappling the opponent's wrist with his own left hand, and executes a right Round House Punch at the other side of the opponent's head.

Grapple, Drag & Ward Off:—

As the opponent is launching a right Straight Forward Punch, Lee's right hand at once grapples the wrist of the opponent's attacking arm, and gives it a downward drag in the same direction as it travels. This renders his opponent to lose balance and tumble forward. At this moment, Lee releases the grappling right hand to launch a heavy Reverse Chopping Punch at the right side of the opponent's face.

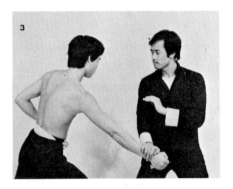
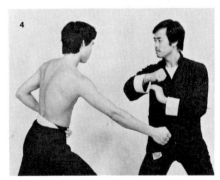

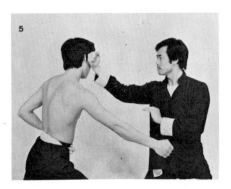

END

"Twelve Flexible Methods"

1. Withdrawing Hands upon Encountering Rigid Movement.
2. Surprise Attack at opponent's unguarded part while he is Attacking.
3. Twirling Around the opponent's Blocking Arm.
4. Gliding Through opponent's Twirling Arm.
5. Deflecting the Straight Forward Punch in accordance with the key-word "Hook".
6. Attacking instantly after the "Pluck" Movement.
7. Attacking with the Other Hand while One Hand is being Grappled.
8. Pressing-in from Outside and Counter-Attack.
9. Attacking instantly after the Downward Pressing Movement.
10. Flipping Off and Attack.
11. Combining the Hands again instantly after the "Open-Arms" blocking movement.
12. Grappling opponent's Arm when it comes into Contact.

十二柔

1	見剛而回手	2	入手而偷手
3	截手而滾手	4	滾手而漏手
5	直統而抅手	6	採手而入手
7	摟手而進手	8	磕手而入手
9	撲手而入手	10	挑手而入手
11	開手而叠手	12	粘手而破手

* Author's note:
As far as theories of the Seven-Star Praying Mantis Style are concerned, the term "YAU" (Flexibility) means a force which is elastic, and, being obstructed, can change its course of travel. It can be applied for both defensive and offensive purposes. It is not, however, applied to counter heavy head-on attack from the opponent, so as to avoid causing both the opponent and the practitioner being wounded. In other words, the application of applying a flexible force aims at "winning over a brute force with an aptly applied force", " avoiding fatal attacks", and "changing one's movement while encountering difficulties".

Withdrawing Hands upon Encountering Rigid Movement:—
When the opponent wants to encounter-attack with powerful rigid movement, the practitioner instantly withdraws his attacking arm to avoid forcible confrontation.

Surprise Attack at opponent's Unguarded Part while he is Attacking:—
While the practitioner sees that his opponent is attempting to attack him, he makes a quick surprise attack at the opponent's unguarded area without bothering to block the opponent's attack directly.

Twirling Around the opponent's Blocking Arm:—
Once the opponent blocks the attacking arm of the practitioner, at this moment he immediately twirls his arm around the opponent's arm to evade his block, then attacks again.

Gliding Through opponent's Twirling Arm:—

If the practitioner blocks the punch of his opponent, and his opponent applies a Twirling Arm to evade the practitioner's block, then the practitioner immediately turns his arm around so as to get out of the control of the Twirling Arm *(B — C)*.   Taking the chance he directly glides his arm through the opponent's Twirling Arm and makes an attack again.

Deflecting the Straight Forward Punch in accordance with the keyword "Hook":--

When an opponent makes an attack to the practitioner, the later applies an Intercept-hand and makes an outward hooking movement to deflect the coming fist so as to nullify the punch. *(P.166 — P. 167)*

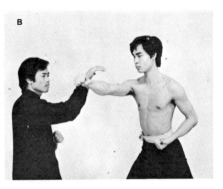

Attacking instantly after the "Pluck" Movement:—

When the opponent attacks with a punch, the practitioner applies, in succession, the techniques of Hook, Grapple, and Pluck, to control the opponent's arm and nullify his attack, (A — D) then immediately after that, the practitioner converts one of his arms into an attacking movement — a Straight Forward Punch or a Straight Forward Palming strike, so as to counter-attack the opponent.

Attacking with the Other Hand while One Hand is being Grappled:—

When the practitioner attacks his opponent with one arm, which is then being controlled, he immediately relaxes this arm of his, to avoid being used as a direction of counter-attack. At the same time he advances to launch attack with the other arm.

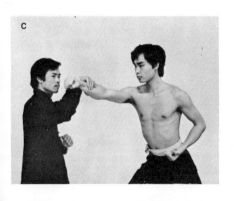

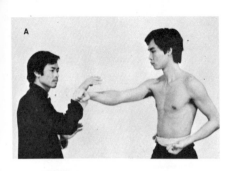

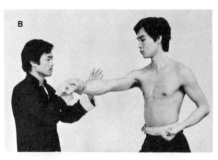

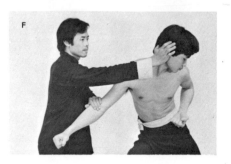

Pressing-in from Outside and Counter-Attack:--

By Pressing-in it means a movement with the arm which comes into the opponent's indoor-area from his outdoor-area, usually aiming to depress the opponent's attacking arm *(B − D)*. After doing this, the practitioner then takes this opportunity to make an counter-attack.

Attacking instantly after the Downward Pressing Movement:--

When the opponent attacks with vigorous punch or punches, the practitioner immediately presses down the attacking arm. He then directly uses the same hand to make a counter-attack. This can also be applied freely by the practitioner if he first presses down his opponent's punch with one hand and tries to counter-attack him with another hand but is soon blocked by the opponent, he then uses the same Downward Pressing Hand to make a surprise attack. *(See illustrations.)*

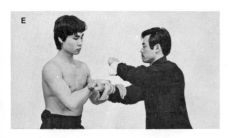

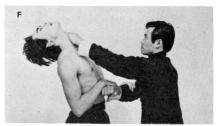

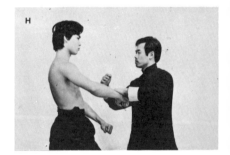

Flipping Off and Attack:--

When the practitioner is being attacked, he immediately blocks the attacking arm and flips it so as to nullify the punch, and then directly makes a counter-attack with the same arm.

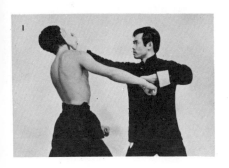

Combining the Hands again instantly after the "Open-Arms" blocking movement:—
When the opponent lauches a Double-palms Movement to attack the practitioner, the latter moves his arms in an outward direction to ward off the strikes. At this movement he instantly combines his opened arms again and counter-attack the opponent.

Grappling opponent's Arm when it comes into Contact:—
This is a way to nullify the grapple by means of the counter-grappling techniques. When the opponent's arm comes into contact with the practitioner's punching arm meaning to grapple it, the practitioner makes a quick counter-grapple of the opponent's arm.

172

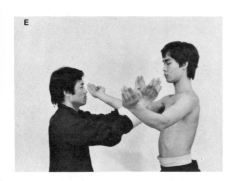

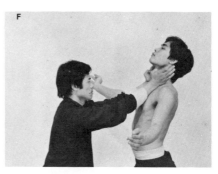

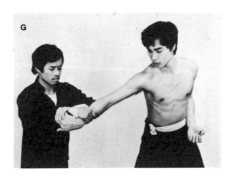
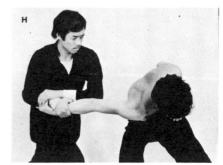

The above verbal formulae imply the main fighting methods of the Seven-Star Praying Mantis Style.

Generally speaking, whenever an opponent adopts a rigid method, the practitioner usually resorts to a flexible method to cope with the opponent's attacks. This is a practical way of allowing the opponent to exhaust his energy while preserving the practitioner's own power.

For attacking purposes, a practitioner would usually use rigid methods for a quick win. The aim is to defeat the opponent with the first launch of attacking movements. In this case, time is an important factor — the more quickly the practitioner delivers his offensive movements, the less prepared for defence would his opponent be, and the sooner the practitioner would secure victory.

The above mentioned methods refer to technical skills in application. For psychological preparation of a practitioner, there are what this system calls *"The Three Conditions of Stability"*, 三 定 which are described as follows: —

"Stability of the Eyesight": —

This means the practitioner should fix his sight on his opponent. His eyesight should in no case be distracted by his environment. He carefully watches what his opponent is doing and what he is going to do. He will never oversee the slightest movement of his opponent. This is what is meant by *"Stability of the Eyes."*

"Stability of the Mind": —

This means the practitioner, while being confronted by his opponent, keeps his mind cool and calm. He refrains from being frightened by his opponent, and does not worry about being defeated at the end. He will not be surprised by sudden changes in his opponent's techniques or tactics.

"Stability of the Stance" —

This means the practitioner keeps a firm stand before his opponent, even though his opponent might be moving from one side of him to the other, or jumping up and down in front of him. The practitioner holds his stance firm, allowing his bodyweight to rest firmly on his lower limbs. He will not aimlessly make a hasty step or jump. Even if he wishes to make a step or a jump, he will keep his own balance. In this way he can always launch heavy attacking movements with his arms.

The *"Three Conditions of Stability"* refer to psychological preparation of a practitioner while he is being confronted by his opponent, but while both have not yet come into fighting contact. The importance lies in getting oneself psychologically prepared — having a firm decision, having confidence in oneself, having no fear, keeping oneself calm, keeping a careful observation of the opponent's movements, keeping away from being distracted or disturbed by any strange or unfamiliar movements of the opponent.

Once contact is being made, a practitioner should then resort to *"The Three Speeds"* — *Speed of the Hands, Speed of the Steps,* and *Speed of the Feet,* in order to defeat his opponent with the first launching of attacks.

In the techniques of the Seven-Star Praying Mantis Style, there are what they call *"The Eight Attacking Points"* and *"The Eight Non-Attacking Points"*. The first group refer to points on the body at which practitioner can attack with an aim to defeat his opponent but without killing him. The second group refer to points on the body at which a practitioner should not attack, because it will bring fatal harm to his opponent or even kill him.

The *Eight Attacking Points* are:

八打

1. The point between the eyes.
2. The center point of the upper lip.
3. The point of the jaw-bone under the eyes.
4. Joints of the spine.
5. The ribs at the two flanks.
6. The pubic bone.
7. The knee-caps and the shins.
8. The collar-bones.

1.打眉頭雙睛
2.打鼻下人中
3.打穿腮耳門
4.打背後骨縫
5.打兩脅肺腑
6.打撩陰高骨
7.打鶴膝虎脛
8.打破骨千斤

* Author's note:
The Eight Attacking Points as described above are based upon the informations supplied by Sifu Lee Kam Wing. However, from the sources of the author's own researches, it turns out that descriptions from different branches of the Northern Praying Mantis Style slightly differ from one and other. For example, the Fifth Attacking Point: "The ribs at the two flanks", should originally be "The lungs' positions of the two flanks", while in some other descriptions, this may read as "joints of the arms".

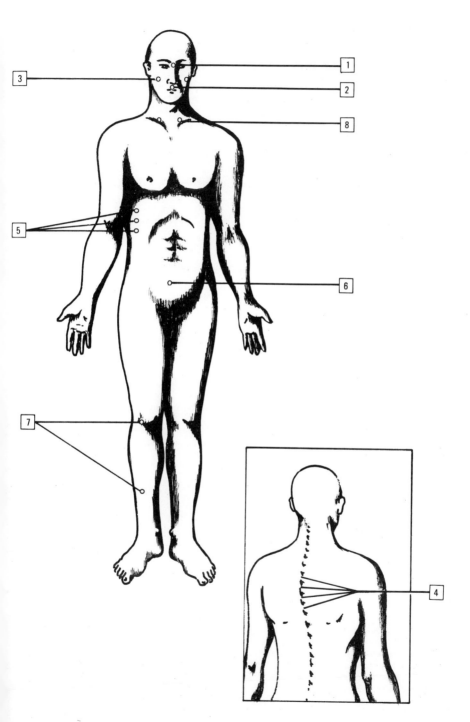

The *Eight Non-Attacking Points* are:

First, not to attack the **Temples of the Head.**

Second, not to attack the **Throat** with the *Mid-throat Lock* Movement.

Third, not to attack the **Center of Back & the Chest.**

Fourth, not attack the **Sides of the Diaphragm.**

Fifth, not to attack the **Scrotum** with the *Groin-Kick.*

Sixth, not to attack the **Kidneys.**

Seventh, not to attack the **Sacrum** & the **junction of the Medulla & spinal cord.**

Eighth, not to attack the **Ears** with the Double-Palm Slapping Movement.

八不打　　1. 不打太陽爲首　　5. 不打海底撩陰
　　　　　 2. 不打正中鎖喉　　6. 不打兩腎對心
　　　　　 3. 不打中心兩壁　　7. 不打尾閭風府
　　　　　 4. 不打兩肋太極　　8. 不打兩耳扇風

The above lethal points are important parts of the body, which, upon being struck, could cause fatal injury or even death. Unless it is a fight for life or death. a practitioner should never attempt striking at these points. The forerunner of the Seven-Star Praying Mantis Style listed these *Eight Attacking Points* and *Eight Non-Attacking Points* so that followers would be able to know where to attack and disable the opponent, and where not to attack to avoid causing death.

* **Author's note:**
The Eight Non-Attacking Points are, similarly, differently described in theories of different branches of the Northern Praying Mantis Style. For example, the explanation of the Fourth Non-Attacking Point, "not to attack the sides of the diaphragm", reads, in descriptions of the other branches, as "not to attack the lungs' positions of the two flanks".

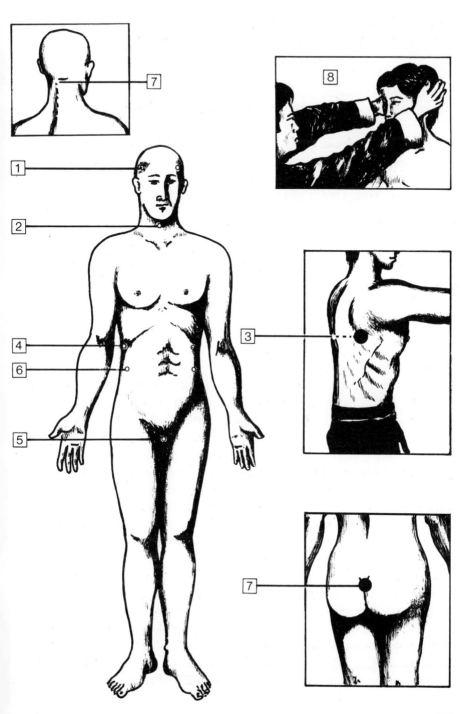

(IV) APPLICATION OF FORCE IN THE SEVEN-STAR PRAYING MANTIS STYLE

(A) Types of Force

There are theoretically two types of forces applicable by a human body.

One is called *"Brute Force"*, which is meant to be that exerted by a man who has never learnt the art of kung fu, such as that applied in daily life, e.g. the force used to move heavy articles, or the force exerted in weight-lifting. This is what is called *"Brute Force"*.

The other kind of force, which can be called *"Dextrous Force"*, is that exerted by a kung fu practitioner. This kind of force cannot be seen from the appearance of the straining muscles or the over emphasized movements of the practitioner, but can only be felt when physical contact with him is made. When applied, this kind of force is extremely destructive.

Generally specking, a brute force is stiffly exerted, while a *"Dextrous Force"* is aptly used. A brute force, once exerted goes straight through its course of travel. On the other hand, a Dextrous Force is elastic and flexible, and when it has been exerted, its strength and course of travel can still be altered as the practitioner wishes. A brute force can only be applied in a mad fight between two angry men, in which, the winner, though having defeated his opponent, is similarly heavily wounded as the loser. A Dextrous Force, on the other hand, is like a sudden explosive power, which injures the enemy in a sudden moment without doing much harm to the practitioner himself. In the application of a force, the higher is the speed, the stronger is the power of destruction; the lower the speed, the weaker the power of destruction. Take a punch for instance. If we use a brute force to launch a punch at our opponent, it can only make a superficial wound on the outer part of him. If, however, a punch is launched at a chosen angle with an aptly applied *Dextrous Force*, it will do the victim a serious internal harm. When an aptly applied *Dextrous Force* is exerted, its power is not visually apparent, but is only sensed by the one who receives such a force. When a brute force is being exerted, the strain on the muscles of the arm that exerts the force is apparent, and can be seen by any on-looker.

It is, therefore, the aptly applied *Dextrous Force,* and not the brute force, which a practitioner of the Seven-Star Praying Mantis Style prefers, and for which he gets training for the highest degree of perfection in applying it. In nature, a force can be *Rigid (YANG)* or *Flexible. (YIN)* A *Rigid Force* is suitable for attacks, or forcible head-on confrontations. A *Flexible Force*, on the other hand, is aptly applied on varying movements to control the opponent's powerful attacking movements. The Seven-Star Praying Mantis Style advocates the use of both kinds of force. There is no standard in the proportion of the use of each kind. Whether to use one or the other in a particular occasion depends on the necessity caused by the techniques adopted by the opponent. In other words, the practitioner decides whether to use a rigid force, or a flexible force, or a combination of the two, to deal with the movements of his opponent, as long as he thinks it is best to do so in that occassion.

(B) Training in the Application of Force
There are three ways of training in applying a force. They are as follows:

(1) The Long Force
This is also know as the *YANG* Force. To launch a punch with such a force, the fist is first kept close to the flank. When a punch is delivered, it is not only the arm that moves. In fact the hind-leg, the waist, the shoulder, the arm and the fist all help to make the punch effective. The force is first generated from the hind-leg, which stretches to make a turning step. The force from the stretching leg is transmitted to the waist, which passes it to the shoulder. From the shoulder, the force is transmitted to the upper-arm and then the fore-arm, The stretching of the whole arm, in a curving course in this case, adds force to that first generated from the hind-leg. The accumulated force is finally passed to the fist, which eventually effectuates when the punch is being stopped by the victim's body. This is how a long force is exerted.

(2) The Foot-length Force
Whilst a long force is generated from the hind-leg, and transmitted through the waist, the shoulder, the whole arm, and finally to the fist, the Foot-length Force, however, is generated from the elbow, and is then transmitted through the fore-arm, the wrist, to the fist. Because of the shorter length of movement, the power is not so great as that

of the Long Force. But the shorter range of a punch delivered by the Foot-length Force makes it a very fast one. Compared with the Inch-length Force, which is the third type of force explained below, the Foot-length Force is longer in its course of delivery. It is the most frequently applied force among the three being discussed.

(3) The Inch-length Force

The Inch-length Force is also known as the *YIN* Force. The force is exerted by the wrist. When a punch is launched, the wrist makes a turn while the force is being exerted to the fist. This kind of force can be applied while at very close range to an opponent, or even in body-contact with him. Because of the confined space in application, it is very difficult to train oneself to master the skills of exerting such a kind of force.

(V) CONCULSION

The techniques of the Northern Seven-Star Praying Mantis Style are a combination of the eighteen forms, which Wang Lang the originator put together to form the present style. These techniques are therefore quite complicated.

Techniques of the Praying Mantis Style include hand methods such as *Hook, Grapple, Pluck, Upward Block, Go forward after Intercept, Chop, Contact, Cling, Tag, Lean,* and foot methods such as *Dodge* and *Bounce*. Besides, there are not only the long range fighting methods, but also close-body fighting techniques, in addition to defending skills such as *Enclosing, Locking,* and *Attaching* on the wrists or other joints of the opponent, and *Throwing* Techniques to deal with various techniques of the opponent.

Because of the variety of techniques of the original Praying Mantis Stule, branches developed as time went on, chiefly as a result of personal attainments and experience of individual students, who added to the original techniques some variations of their own.

Therefore, there are now branch styles such as the **Dragging Hand Praying Mantis Style**, which stresses on methods of *enclosing the opponent, short range punches, Grappling* and *Dragging* techniques etc.; the **Eight-Step Praying Mantis**, which emphasizes on steps and positioning, and techniques such as *Dodging, Turning, Bouncing* and *Moving about*; the **Rigid Praying Mantis**, which advocates the use of vigorous and rigid movements; the **Six Combinations Praying Mantis** and the **Tai Chi Praying Mantis**, both of which prefer using flexible techniques, making use of the opponent's force to defeat the opponent himself, and ways of neutralizing the opponent's attacking force; the **Flat Plate Praying Mantis**. which aims primarily at using palm methods; the **Leg-Detecting Praying Mantis**, which stresses on the employment of footworks and kicking; and the **Plum Blossom Praying Mantis**, which is famous for its upper-level and mid-level hand techniques. As for the **Seven-Star Praying Mantis Style**, it is the *Seven-Star Steps*, in which the style excels.

One common characteristic of all the Praying Mantis Styles is that the hand movements are always followed by the steps. The *TIAO-SHAO*, or the **Intercept-hand** closely resembles the foreleg of the mantis. Steps adopted by the Praying Mantis Styles are those called the *"Monkey Steps"*, which allows the practitioner *to jump, to advance, retreat, or evade* easily and quickly. Special steps adopted by the Seven-Star Praying Mantis Style are called the *"Seven-Star Steps"*. Of other techniques, this style advocates balanced development of techniques for all the *three levels*. As for boxing forms, there are altogether over 40 forms, with each form bearing its respective characteristics. Weapons adopted by the Seven-Star Praying Mantis Style are numerous in number, ranging from very short weapons, such as the dagger, to long ones, such as the long spear, the long-handle broadsword, the long halberd; and heavy weapons like the brass global-headed double-hammer, and many other kinds, which can't be described in detail here.

Amongst all the hand techniques used by practitioners of the Seven-Star Praying Mantis Style, *the Intercept-hand* is most frequently employed. The *Intercept-hand* technique can be changed to a series of successive techniques such as *Hook, Grapple,* and then *Pluck,* which together form a chain of movements which offer defense and counter-attack at the same time. Besides, an *Intercept-hand* can be converted to the individual grappling hand to co-ordinate with movements of the other hand. Or, alternatively, it can perform a joint movement on its own, by first intercepting *(deflecting the coming punch by means of Hook or grappling the opponent's arm)*, and, immediately after that, counter-attacking in the form of a punch *(The joint-movement of the keywords "OU-LOU-TSAI")*. The versatility in the use of the *Intercept-hand*, and the varieties of hand techniques which it can give rise to, make it the most frequently employed technique when a practitioner encounters an opponent.

As a matter of fact, techniques of the Seven-Star Praying Mantis Style are not totally rigid, nor are they entirely flexible. There is actually flexibility in the application of the rigid movements of this style of kung fu, and rigidity is also found in the manpulation of flexible movements. Generally specking, the techniques of the Seven-Star Praying Mantis Style are not so rigid as those of the Rigid Praying Mantis Style, but a little more rigid than those of the Six Combinations Praying Mantis Style.

As regards punching methods, the Seven-Star Praying Mantis Style weighs on the **Straight Forward Punch** *(which is particularly frequently used in Sifu Lee Kam Wing's system).* In this punch, the fist goes straight forward at mid-level height, while during the travel of the fist, that is, from the moment when the force is exerted to the moment the fist comes into contact with the victim's body, a kind of *"spiraling force"* is being generated, which is similar to that caused by the bullet passing through the barrel of the gun. This force causes the fist to go faster, and makes the punch more powerful. This punch is best employed to attack the front part of the opponent, from the forehead, the face, the neck, the chest down to the abdomen.

There are punches such as the *"Head-on Chopping Fist"*, which is a vigorous downward punch, and the *"Slant Chopping Fist"*, which goes from the upper left side to the lower right side, or vice versa. The above two kinds of punches are extremely heavy, and are applied for attacking important parts of the opponent, such as the head and the neck. They are equally frequent in use by practitioners of the Seven-Star Praying Mantis Style.

Palming techniques are also widely applied in the Seven-Star Praying Mantis Style. Comparatively speaking, a punch is more vigorous and powerful in application, while a palming attack is more flexible and easily controlled in application. Because of the difference in force application, a punch is more suitable to be employed in apparent attacks, but has the disadvantage of being difficult to apply well within short ranges. A palming attack, on the other hand, driven with a force usually generated from the wrist, can be applied at a very short distance from the opponent, and has the advantage of being able to be executed from a position and at an angle usually neglected by the opponent. Thus a palming attack can always be launched to the surprise of the opponent, while a punch is too obvious to take an opponent by surprise. This is the difference between the punching and the palming techniques.

It is generally far more difficult to apply a palming technique than to apply a punch. In applying a punch the point of contact is meant to be the bony part of fore-fist of the hand, with which even a beginner or a layman can easily wound the victim. But, compared to the fist, the palm is much softer, being more fleshy and flexible. Though there are methods such as the *"Thrusting Palm"*, which makes an attack with the tip of

1. Straight Forward Punch.
2. Sideway Horizontal Straight Punch.
3. Slant Chopping Fist.
4. Sideway Straight Forward Punch.

6. Head-on Chopping Fist.

5. Twisting Straight Punch.

186

the flattened palm, yet a palming attack is on more occassions less destructive than punches. This is true at least for beginners, or for those who are not expertised at the use of the palm. Therefore, unless a practitioner is well advanced in his techniques, he can hardly wound his opponent with his palm. This explains why a palming technique is more difficult to apply than a punch.

1. Stamping Palm.

2. Waist Chopping Palm.

3. Master Lee is applying the left hand as the Thrusting Palm, while the right one as the Slapping Palm.

5. Application of the Reverse Palm.

4. Horizontal Chopping Palm.

There are several methods of palming attacks in the Seven-Star Praying Mantis Style. One method is to use the centre of the palm for attacking purposes. Another method is to attack the opponent by thrusting the four straightened fingers of the palm at the opponent, in the form of a *"Thrusting Palm"*. Another method is to chop horizontally at the opponent, in which case the point of contact is the side of the palm. This is what is known as the *"Horizontal Chop"*, or the *"Waist Chop"*. Still another is to use the back of the palm to attack the opponent, in the fashion of a *"Reverse Palm"*. There is also a method of putting the palm together to launch a cutting attack at the joints of the opponent's arms, which is termed the *"Joint Cutting Palm"*.

The single palm or joined palms may be use to sweep to block, or to cut at the arms of an opponent. Palm attacks may also be executed by combining several palming fashions for simultaneous defensive and offensive purposes, such as the *"Grinding Palm"*, the *"Great Whirl-Stamping Palm"*, and the *"Little Whirl-Stamping Palm"* etc.

Kicking methods with the legs and feet are numerous in the Seven-Star Praying Mantis Style. These kicking methods are classified into two groups, namely the *"Leg-Kicks"* and the *"Foot-Kicks"*. A leg-kick is a large action, and can be applied for attacking a larger area of the opponent. It is thus more apparent, and needs the help of co-ordination of the body to launch. A foot-kick is comparatively a smaller action. The area of the wound of the victim is comparatively smaller but the attack is more precise. The attack of a foot-kick is tricky and more difficult to avoid.

Nowadays, however, the difference between leg-kicks and foot-kicks is very often confused by followers of many Praying Mantis Styles, and the above descriptions of leg-kicks and foot-kicks do not necessarily represent the theories of all Northern Praying Mantis Styles.

Target Areas of attack with leg-kicks are normally directed at three parts of the victim's body: *the upper-level, the mid-level* and *the lower-level*. For attacking the upper-level, a leg-kick is often co-ordinated with vaults or jumps. These large movements are good-looking, but movements that appear to be beautiful are not always practicable. Therefore in real application they are not very often applied, unless occasions make them necessary and feasible. Leg-kicks at the mid-level and the lower-level are smaller movements. They could usually give little influence to the balance of the practitioner's body. And because these kicks are very often applied under the cover of arm movements, they are more frequently used.

1. **The "Whirl Kick".** *(A Leg-Kick Technique)*
2. **Foot-Stamping Kick.** *(A Foot-Kick Technique)*
3. **Groin-Kick.** *(A Leg-Kick Technique)*
4. **Stamping Kick to the Knee-cap.** *(A Foot-Kick Technique)*
5. **Sweeping Kick to the Shin.** *(A Foot-Kick Technique)*

Techniques with the fingers, the elbow, and the knee are very often employed in the Seven-Star Praying Mantis Style.

Fingers are usually applied for thrusting at the eyes and the throat, or for choking the throat of the opponent. Fingers can also be used to claw at the face of the opponent.

1. **Double-Finger Strike to the eyes.**
2. **Thrusting Palm to the kidney position of the waist.** *(* The Thrusting Palm Technique can be strictly regarded as Fingers Technique)*
3. **Throat-Locking Hand Technique.**
4. **Application of the "Claw".**

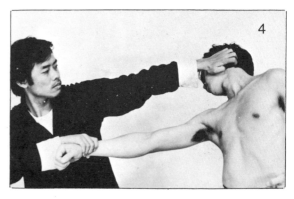

Elbow or knee attacks are usually applied at close range to the opponent, or at body contact with him. A sudden elbow attack or knee attack at a suitable moment will usually bring a quick wounding effect on an opponent. The elbow, being hard· and pointed, and at close range to an opponent, can very often effectuate an attack, which is very difficult to avoid. A knee attack can only take place when the opponent is close enough. The area of attack with the knee is usually the crutch of the opponent, or his abdomen. These parts are the weak points of the human body. Besides, a practitioner can also use his knee to block a coming kick, if it can be applied at a favourable angle, or to butt at the side or the back of the leg, or the calf. This will usually partially disable the opponent's leg, or at least to nullify his kick.

1. Sideway Elbow Strike.
2. Joint-Breaking Technique with the Elbow.
3. Application of the Sideway Elbow Strike.
4. Application of the Knee Strike Technique.

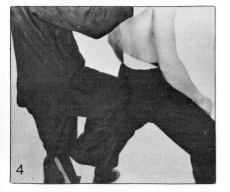

Amongst the tactics employed by practitioners of the Seven-Star Praying Mantis Style, there is one which can be termed *"Shadow Punch"*, which is a feigning movement with one arm to distract the opponent's attention, while the practitioner launches a quick attack with the other arm. Because the opponent is busy dealing with the feigning movement, he is often taken in by the practitioner's real attacking movement.

There is a motto, which reads, "Feign at the upper part, and attack the lower part; feign at the lower part, and attack the upper part; feign at the left side, and attack the right side; feign at the right side, and attack the left side".

Feigning movements do not confine to the arms only. They can also be applied with the legs. Sometimes arms and legs may co-operate in making feigning movements for attacking purposes.

An example of this is when a practitioner is confronted by his opponent, who is standing in front of him. The practitioner feigns an attack at the upper-level of the opponent with an arm. The opponent would usually try to defend his upper-level. At this moment, the practitioner suddenly launches a kick at his opponent's lower–level. This is what is meant by "Feign at the upper part, and attack the lower part".

Besides, a practitioner, on certain occasions, can also feign a kick at the mid-level or lower-level of the opponent, making him busy in setting up defense for his mid-level or lower-level, while at this moment the practitioner launches a heavy punch at the opponent's head. This is what is meant by "Feign at the lower part, and attack the upper part".

Therefore, in the theories of the Seven-Star Praying Mantis Style, there is the following saying:

"To take the upper part, first feign at the lower; to cut the lower part, first feign at the upper. To attack the left, be aware of the right; to attack the right, be aware of the left. Take care of both the upper and the lower parts; correlate the left and the right. Block and then attack at the first instance; attack and then block at the first instance. Defense should be accompanied by attacking movement; attack should be accompanied by defensive movement. It is an expert who wins without blocking in advance; and it is an outsider who knows only blocking the opponent but not to attack.''

END

DIAGRAM OF THE TERMS OF POSITIONS

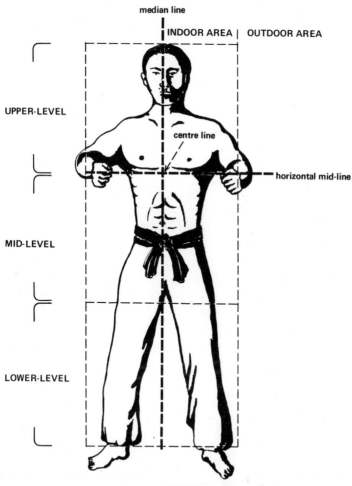

In Chinese terminology the two arms of the body are equivalent to two leaves of door. When both arms are out stretched, the area embraced by both arms or between the inner part of both arms is called the indoor area, while the area beyond the outer part of both arms is called the outdoor area.

* The traditional Chinese door has two leaves which open inwards.